W0036683

Oxford Skills World

Listening 5

WITH Speaking

Jessica Finnis

OXFORD
UNIVERSITY PRESS

OXFORD
UNIVERSITY PRESS

198 Madison Avenue
New York, NY 10016 USA

Great Clarendon Street, Oxford, OX2 6DP, United Kingdom

Oxford University Press is a department of the University of Oxford.
It furthers the University's objective of excellence in research, scholarship,
and education by publishing worldwide. Oxford is a registered trade
mark of Oxford University Press in the UK and in certain other countries

ISBN: 978 0 19 411342 7 STUDENT BOOK WITH WORKBOOK

Printed in Great Britain by Bell and Bain Ltd, Glasgow

This book is printed on paper from certified and well-managed sources

ACKNOWLEDGMENTS

Cover illustration and main character illustrations by: Shane McGowan/The
Organisation

Cover photograph: Thomas Zagler/123rf

Back cover photograph: Oxford University Press building/David Fisher

Student Book

Illustrations by: Scott Angle pp.9–10, 44, 82–83; Mattia Cerato/MB Artists p.54;
Peter Francis/MB Artists p.22; Leslie Harrington pp.8, 36, 78; 5W Infographics
p.64; Chris Jones/Maggie Byers Sprinzeles pp.41–42, 88; Anthony Lewis/
MB Artists pp.30, 84; Juan Moreno/MB Artists pp.16, 74; Christos Skaltsas/
Advocate Art pp.27–28, 72; Jomike Tejido/MB Artists pp.55, 69

*The Publishers would like to thank the following for their kind permission to reproduce
photographs and other copyright material*: 123rf: pp.12 (planting flowers/Alexander
Raths), 15 (girl gardening/Mykola Velychko), 29 (woodland in fall/sborisov),
45 (shopping list/belchonock), 50 (white feather/foodandmore), 58 (rhino
running/Andrew Deer), 64 (sheep in field/Klanarong Chitmung), (mountain
range/Galyna Andrushko), 66 (hello poster/Robert Wilson), 68 (old castle/
Catherine Jones), 71 (palace of versailles/Chan Richie); Alamy: pp.15 (planting
seeds/Elizabeth Whiting & Associates), 18 (girl with sunflower/Juice Images),
81 (cat shaped money box/YAY Media AS), 86 (earth ship tire wall/Les.
Ladbury); Getty: pp.6–7 (boys washing up/Hero Images), 11 (man with wheelie
bin/Moxie Productions), 12 (drying a plate/Jamie Grill), 15 (family washing up/
Steve Debenport), (three boys on laptop/Hero Images), 24 (girl sledding/Ariel
Skelley), 26 (family around fire/Ariel Skelley), 30 (children body boarding/
Clarissa Leahy), 37 (food festival/robertcicchetti), 39 (child cooking/MIXA next),
40 (yogurt and spoon/George Doyle), 54 (two pandas in tree/Hung_Chung_
Chih), 59 (two people taking photos/Corbis/VCG), 69 (father and child reading/
ULTRA.F), 79 (child picking litter/Chad Springer), 86 (eco house/helovi),
87 (man and dog/Maksym Azovtsev); Oxford University Press: pp.12 (watering
plants/Shutterstock/Denis and Yulia Pogostins), (planting seeds/Shutterstock/
amenic181), 26 (snowflake/Shutterstock/Kichigin), (ice cube melting/
Shutterstock/r.classen), 29 (bucket and spade/Shutterstock), (mountains/
Shutterstock/Pichugin Dmitry), 32 (coastline/123rf/sergein), 40 (cinnnamon
sticks/Shutterstock/Oliver Hoffmann), 50 (peacock displaying feathers/
Shutterstock/percom), 52 (hummingbird/Shutterstock/Ondrej Prosicky),
53 (eagle flying/Shutterstock/visceralimage), 68 (skyline at night/Shutterstock/
pcruciatti), 71 (canals in venice/Shutterstock/Catarina Belova); Shutterstock:
pp.8 (clothes in washing machine/Kalcutta), (clothes drying on line/Delpixel),
12 (family gardening/wavebreakmedia), 13 (hands holding garland/wirakorn
deelert), 14 (present/Pixel Embargo), 17 (girl and boy watering flowers/waldru),
20–21 (fish and reef/Brian Kinney), 22 (children sledding/Rawpixel.com),
23 (two girls talking/gpointstudio), 25 (beach/David MG), 26 (raking leaves/
Africa Studio), (picking an apple/JP Chretien), (icicles/intoit), 29 (family around
fire/Syda Productions), 31 (hands on laptop/Georgejmclittle), 34–35 (banana
plant/vincentchuls), 36 (kimchi/norikko), 38 (lady serving food/ployypoii),
40 (honey and yogurt/Peredniankina), (spinach leaves/Jiri Hera), (three chili
peppers/Kateryna Bibro), 43 (range of spices/Alexei), (mother and daughter
cooking/Kokulina), (shopping at a supermarket/Monkey Business Images),
(shopping at a market/William Perugini), 44 (frog carved from watermelon/
PP_photography), 46 (pizza/gkrphoto), 48–49 (two tigers playing/Onkar
Sansare), 50 (flamingo/Independent Birds), (flamingo head/AOME1812),
(eagle beak/LukaKikina), 51 (peacock feathers/Yuliya Koldovska), (two swans/
Algirdas Gelazius), 53 (two peacocks/PeterVrabel), (group of flamingos/Kirill
Dorofeev), (close of up peacock feather/Chursina Viktoriia), 56 (two pandas
on ground/df028), 57 (help protect logo/Fejas), 58 (tiger and a jeep/Dr Ajay
Kumar Singh), (roller in flight/PhotocechCZ), (tiger print in sand/diy13),
60 (penguins/vladsilver), 62–63 (busy street/BABAROGA), 64 (red square in
the snow/Pavel L Photo and Video), (tower of london/Alexander Chaikin),
65 (village elders/Kertu), 67 (someone using a smartphone/Vasin Lee),
68 (grand palace Bangkok./Travel mania), (passport/piaharrisphotography),
(japanese food/hiphoto), 70 (post it notes on table/Rido), 71 (grand bazaar in
istanbul/Luciano Mortula-LGM), (family on a beach/Monkey Business Images),
72 (Tsaritsyno Palace in Moscow./Dance60), 73 (Russian dolls/Veniamin
Kraskov), 76–77 (litter in countryside/Andriy Solovyov), 78 (wodden toy box/
Mikhail Rulkov), 80 (campsite in woods/shutter_o), 82 (girls whispering/Tom
Wang), (plate of chips/Jacek Chabraszewski), (broken glass/r.classen), (cotton
plant/ConstantinosZ), 85 (white shirt/Suradech Prapairat), (stainless steel pans/
Delpixel), (vase of flowers/Africa Studio), (waterfall/Greg Browning), 86 (inside
of eco house/Takako Picture Lab), (glass house/Larysa_Geoffrey Moler)

Workbook

Illustrations by: Scott Angle p.113; Leslie Harrington p.97; Anthony Lewis/MB
Artists p.91; Juan Moreno/MB Artists p.105; Jomike Tejido/MB Artists pp.101,
109

*The Publishers would like to thank the following for their kind permission to reproduce
photographs and other copyright material*: Alamy: p.93 (Asian family/WizData
inc.); Oxford University Press: pp.95 (palm tree and beach/Shutterstock/Anton
Gvozdikov), 96 (tropical beach/Shutterstock/Efired), 100 (mixed fruit and veg/
Shutterstock/stocker1970), 108 (national flags/Shutterstock/Markus Pfaff),
112 (plastic bottle/Shutterstock); Shutterstock: pp.92 (laundry bin/Aerostato),
99 (female doctor/SuperStockShots), 103 (eagle flying with fish/Menno
Schaefer), 107 (path through forest/Naruedom Taempongsa), 111 (flowers
made from trash/Elizaveta Galitckaia)

Table of Contents

Hi! I'm Olly.

Hi, I'm Molly!

Introduction

Welcome to Oxford Skills World

Oxford Skills World: Listening with Speaking is a flexible paired skills course that takes students on a journey toward independent learning, providing them with strategies and support to reach their goals.

For Students

- Student Book / Workbook
- Student's website with downloadable audio and extra resources
  www.oup.com/elt/oxfordskillsworld

For Teachers

- Downloadable Teacher's Pack with instructional support, assessment, professional development videos, projects, and speaking resources
- Classroom Presentation Tool
- Teacher's website with downloadable audio and extra resources
  www.oup.com/elt/teacher/oxfordskillsworld

Be the Leader on Your Skills Adventure!

Hi! We're Olly and Molly, your skills adventure guides. We help you reach your goals by introducing new listening and speaking strategies, asking helpful questions, and giving friendly reminders. Most importantly, we cheer you on every step of the way! Let's go!

Quick Guide

Inside Each Topic

Topic Opener

Theme-based topics provide high-interest content relevant to students' lives.

My Goals introduces students to the objectives of each unit in the topic.*

Students answer questions to activate prior knowledge and think critically.

Students listen to a Fun Fact to increase their engagement with the topic.

Fun characters, Olly and Molly, encourage 21st century skills like critical thinking, collaboration, and communication.

Get Ready to Listen • Listen

Students learn and practice new vocabulary. They can look up unknown words in a dictionary at the back of the book.

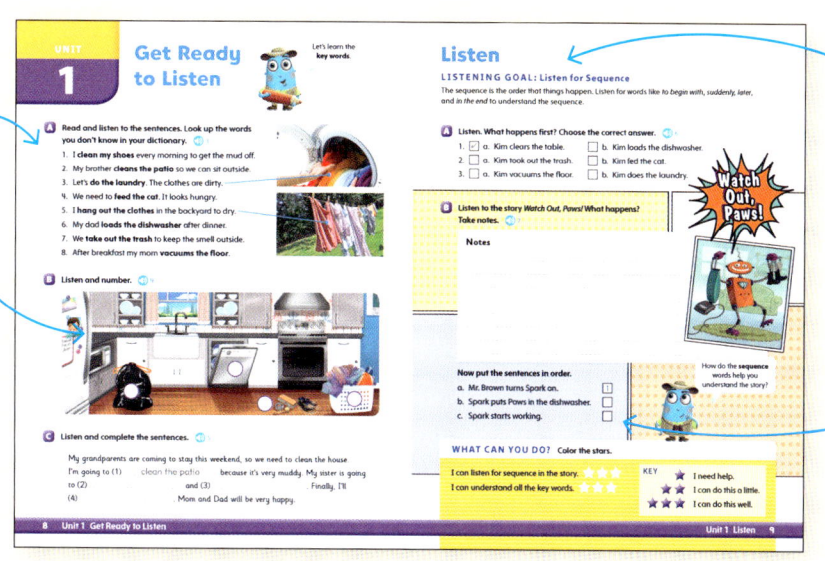

Listening Goals are strategies students can apply to any passage.

Students apply strategies to high-interest fiction and nonfiction passages, think critically about what they hear, and make connections to their own lives.

*Each topic contains two thematically related units.

Quick Guide

Understand

Students increase their comprehension of the passages by applying listening strategies to what they have heard.

Students complete activities focused on listening comprehension and critical thinking.

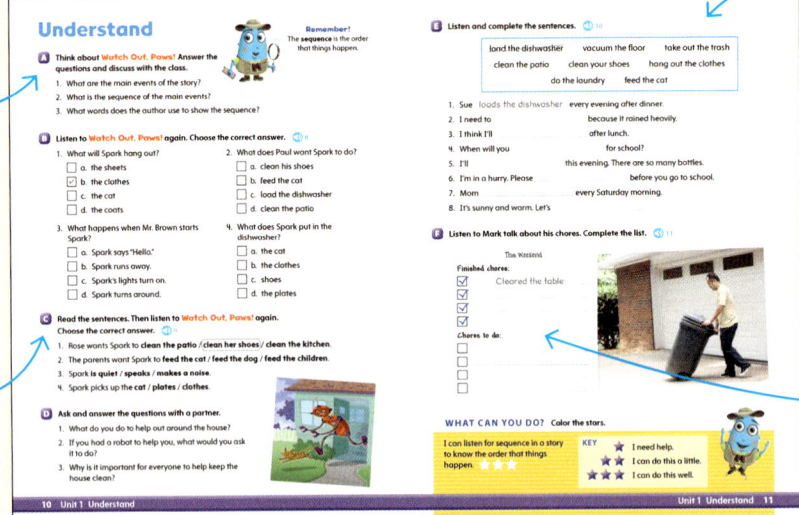

Vocabulary application activities strengthen students' comprehension of the unit's new language.

Additional passages and activities prepare students for task types found on standardized exams, such as Cambridge English Qualifications for young learners.

Listening Check

With helpful reminders from Olly and Molly, students apply the **Listening Goals** from both units to a new passage.

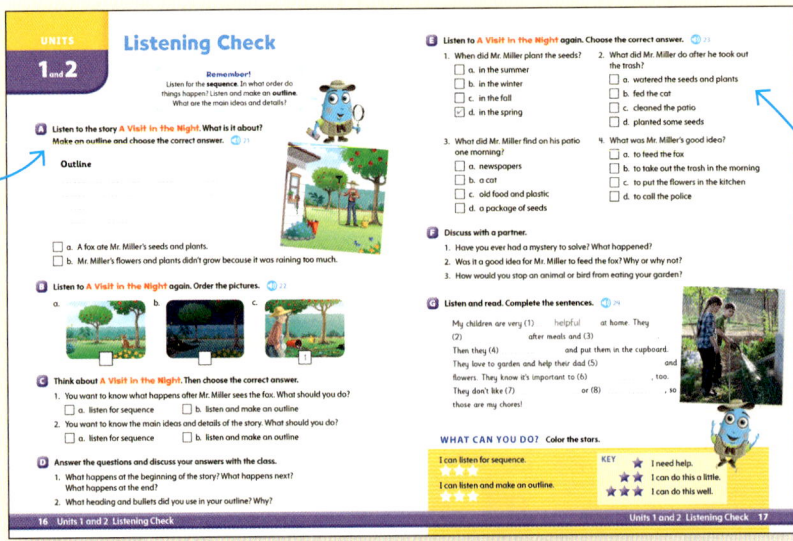

Students complete activities to boost listening comprehension and vocabulary application.

Get Ready to Speak • Speak

Speaking Goals prepare students to speak in different contexts.

Speaking Tips provide guidance on grammar, punctuation, and mechanics and help students speak fluently and accurately.

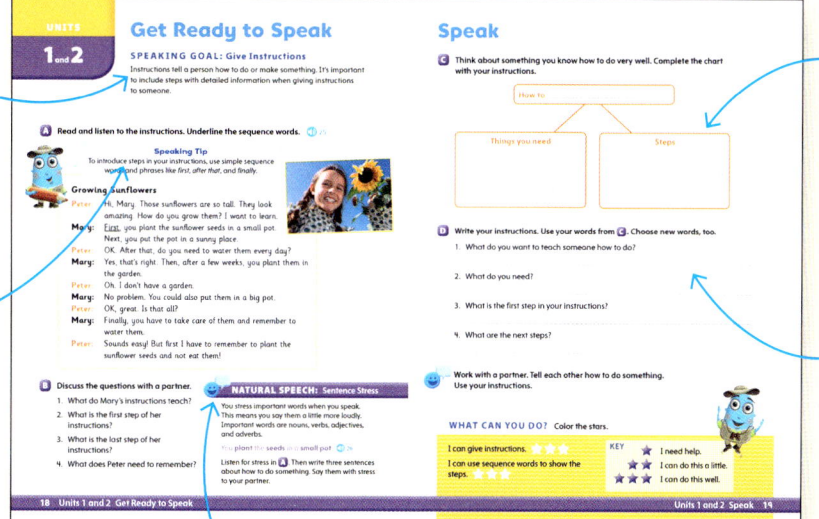

Students use graphic organizers to organize their thoughts for their own speaking.

Thought-provoking questions help students generate ideas they will use in their own speaking.

Natural Speech tips help students listen for and use natural rhythm, pronunciation, and intonation.

Workbook

Workbook pages at the end of the book provide more opportunities for students to apply their **Listening Goals** and boost comprehension.

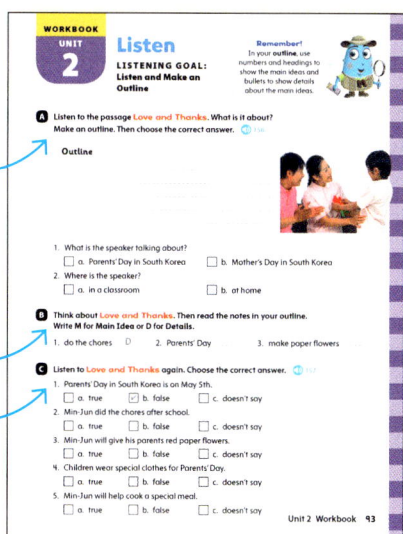

Additional activities provide extra opportunities for listening comprehension and vocabulary practice.

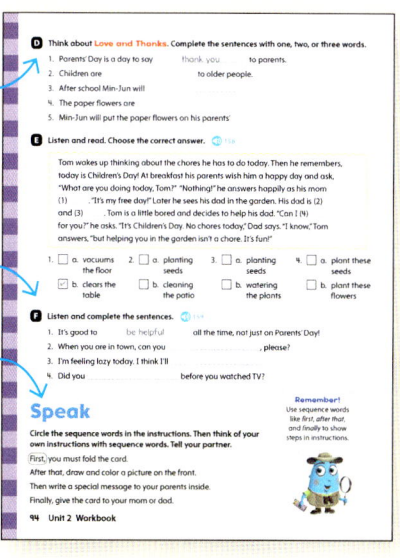

Students apply the topic's **Speaking Tip** to ensure proper usage in their own speaking.

TOPIC

1

SOCIAL STUDIES

Helping Out

MY GOALS

UNIT 1

- Listen to the story *Watch Out, Paws!*
- Listen for sequence

UNIT 2

- Listen to the conversation *A Special Day in Thailand*
- Listen and make an outline

SPEAK

- Give instructions

 Look at the picture.

1. Where are the children? What are they doing?
2. Who does this chore in your house?

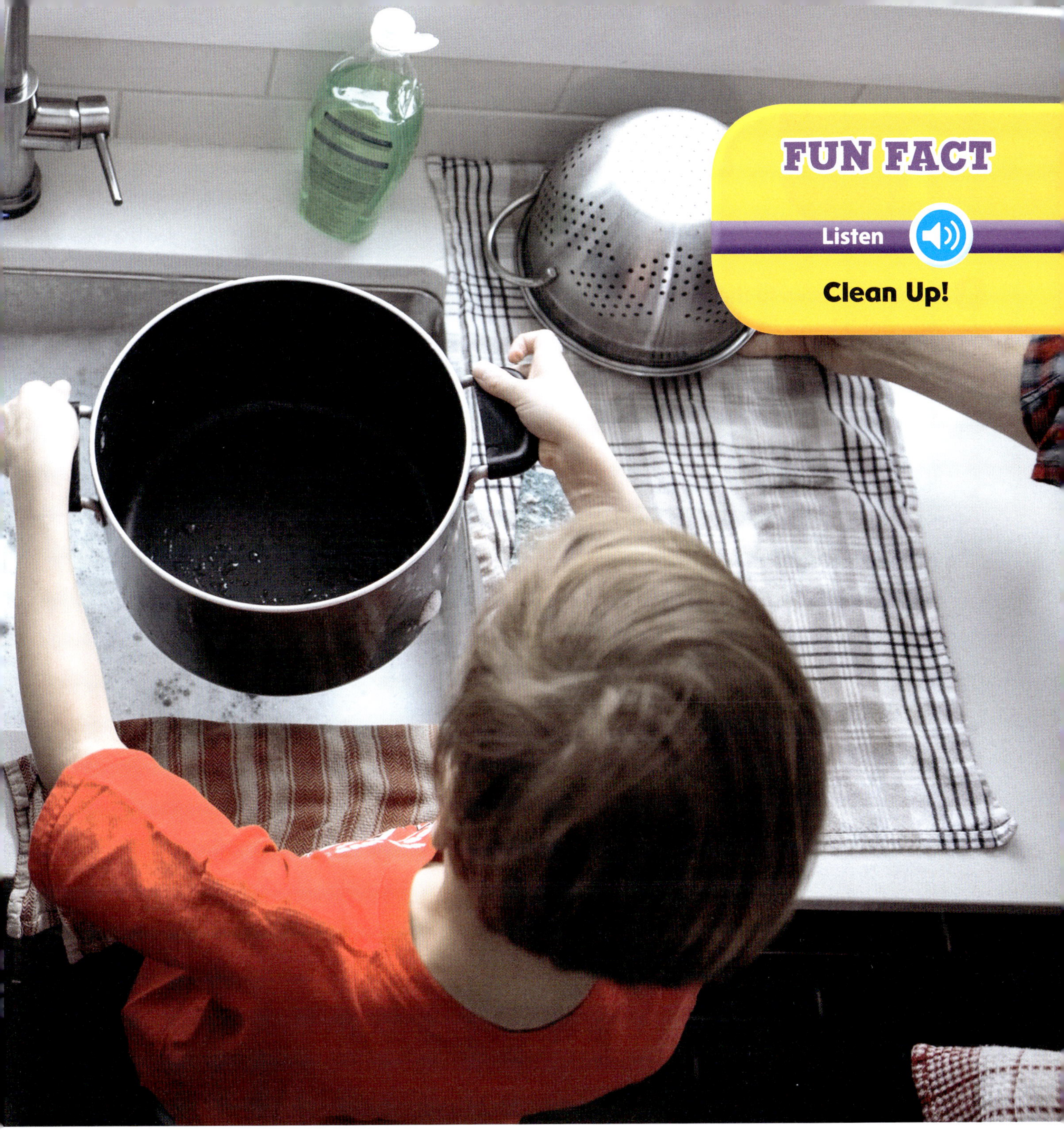

FUN FACT

Listen

Clean Up!

B Listen to the Fun Fact. Then answer the questions. 2

1. How much of their lives do people spend doing chores?
2. How many people enjoy doing chores?
3. What chores do you enjoy doing?

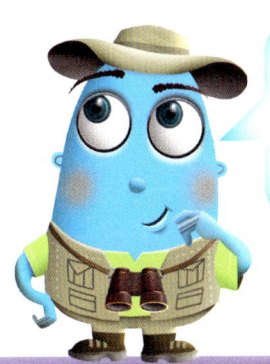

Think, Pair, Share
How much time do you spend doing chores each day?

Get Ready to Listen

Let's learn the **key words**.

A Read and listen to the sentences. Look up the words you don't know in your dictionary. 🔊 3

1. I **clean my shoes** every morning to get the mud off.
2. My brother **cleans the patio** so we can sit outside.
3. Let's **do the laundry**. The clothes are dirty.
4. We need to **feed the cat**. It looks hungry.
5. I **hang out the clothes** in the backyard to dry.
6. My dad **loads the dishwasher** after dinner.
7. We **take out the trash** to keep the smell outside.
8. After breakfast my mom **vacuums the floor**.

B Listen and number. 🔊 4

C Listen and complete the sentences. 🔊 5

My grandparents are coming to stay this weekend, so we need to clean the house. I'm going to (1) _____clean the patio_____ because it's very muddy. My sister is going to (2) _____ and (3) _____. Finally, I'll (4) _____. Mom and Dad will be very happy.

Listen

The sequence is the order that things happen. Listen for words like *to begin with*, *suddenly, later,* and *in the end* to understand the sequence.

A **Listen. What happens first? Choose the correct answer.** 🔊 6

1. ☑ a. Kim clears the table. ☐ b. Kim loads the dishwasher.
2. ☐ a. Kim took out the trash. ☐ b. Kim fed the cat.
3. ☐ a. Kim vacuums the floor. ☐ b. Kim does the laundry.

B **Listen to the story *Watch Out, Paws!* What happens? Take notes.** 🔊 7

Notes

Watch Out, Paws!

How do the **sequence** words help you understand the story?

Now put the sentences in order.

a. Mr. Brown turns Spark on. `1`

b. Spark puts Paws in the dishwasher. ☐

c. Spark starts working. ☐

WHAT CAN YOU DO? Color the stars.

I can listen for sequence in the story. ★★★

I can understand all the key words. ★★★

KEY ★ I need help.

★★ I can do this a little.

★★★ I can do this well.

Understand

Remember!
The **sequence** is the order that things happen.

A Think about **Watch Out, Paws!** Answer the questions and discuss with the class.

1. What are the main events of the story?

2. What is the sequence of the main events?

3. What words does the author use to show the sequence?

B Listen to **Watch Out, Paws!** again. Choose the correct answer. 🔊 8

1. What will Spark hang out?
   - [ ] a. the sheets
   - [✔] b. the clothes
   - [ ] c. the cat
   - [ ] d. the coats

2. What does Paul want Spark to do?
   - [ ] a. clean his shoes
   - [ ] b. feed the cat
   - [ ] c. load the dishwasher
   - [ ] d. clean the patio

3. What happens when Mr. Brown starts Spark?
   - [ ] a. Spark says "Hello."
   - [ ] b. Spark runs away.
   - [ ] c. Spark's lights turn on.
   - [ ] d. Spark turns around.

4. What does Spark put in the dishwasher?
   - [ ] a. the cat
   - [ ] b. the clothes
   - [ ] c. shoes
   - [ ] d. the plates

C Read the sentences. Then listen to **Watch Out, Paws!** again. Choose the correct answer. 🔊 9

1. Rose wants Spark to **clean the patio** / clean her shoes / **clean the kitchen**.

2. The parents want Spark to **feed the cat** / **feed the dog** / **feed the children**.

3. Spark **is quiet** / **speaks** / **makes a noise**.

4. Spark picks up the **cat** / **plates** / **clothes**.

D Ask and answer the questions with a partner.

1. What do you do to help out around the house?

2. If you had a robot to help you, what would you ask it to do?

3. Why is it important for everyone to help keep the house clean?

E Listen and complete the sentences. 🔊 10

> load the dishwasher   vacuum the floor   take out the trash
>
> clean the patio   clean your shoes   hang out the clothes
>
> do the laundry   feed the cat

1. Sue _loads the dishwasher_ every evening after dinner.

2. I need to _____ because it rained heavily.

3. I think I'll _____ after lunch.

4. When will you _____ for school?

5. I'll _____ this evening. There are so many bottles.

6. I'm in a hurry. Please _____ before you go to school.

7. Mom _____ every Saturday morning.

8. It's sunny and warm. Let's _____

F Listen to Mark talk about his chores. Complete the list. 🔊 11

This Weekend

Finished chores:

✓ Cleared the table
✓ _____
✓ _____
✓ _____

Chores to do:

☐ _____
☐ _____
☐ _____
☐ _____

WHAT CAN YOU DO?   Color the stars.

I can listen for sequence in a story to know the order that things happen.

KEY   I need help.

 I can do this a little.

I can do this well.

Get Ready to Listen

Let's learn the **key words**.

A Read and listen to the sentences. Look up the words you don't know in your dictionary. 🔊 12

1. After dinner Tom **clears the table**.

2. After washing the dishes, we **dry the dishes** with a towel.

3. My brother is very **helpful**. He checks my homework for me.

4. She went to the post office to **mail a package**.

5. Let's **plant seeds** in the garden and see what flowers grow.

6. We are **planting flowers**. It's spring so they grow fast.

7. Sue **stays at home** each night to do her homework.

8. It's important to **water the plants** so they grow.

B Listen and write the number under the picture. 🔊 13

a. ____   b. ____   c. _1_   d. ____

C Read each sentence. Then listen to the words. Two of the three key words are incorrect. Write the correct key word. 🔊 14

1. This is what you do after washing the plates.   dry the dishes

2. You do this every few days to help plants grow.   _____

3. You need to do this to send a present to a friend. _____

4. If you are sick, it's best to do this.   _____

Listen

LISTENING GOAL: Listen and Make an Outline

Outlining is a form of note-taking. In an outline, use numbers and headings to show main ideas. Then use bullet points to show details about the main ideas.

A Listen and complete the outlines. 🔊 15

1. **Inside chores**
   - clear the table
   - _____

2. **Outside chores**
   - _____
   - _____

A Special Day in Thailand

B Listen to the conversation *A Special Day in Thailand*. What is it about? Make an outline with main ideas and details. 🔊 16

Outline

_____
_____
_____
_____
_____

Now read. Choose **T** for **True** or **F** for **False**.

1. Pom is talking about Mother's Day.   (T)   F
2. Pom is talking about chores she did.   T   F
3. Pom is not doing anything special this evening.   T   F

How does an **outline** help you remember what you hear?

WHAT CAN YOU DO?   Color the stars.

I can listen to a conversation and make an outline.

I can understand all the key words.

KEY

⭐ I need help.
⭐⭐ I can do this a little.
⭐⭐⭐ I can do this well.

Understand

A Think about **A Special Day in Thailand**. Answer the questions and discuss with the class.

1. What are the headings in your outline? Why?

2. What details did you include in your outline?

3. Do you need to include every detail in an outline? Why or why not?

4. Was it helpful to make an outline? Why or why not?

B Listen to **A Special Day in Thailand** again. Choose **T** for **True** or **F** for **False**. 17

1. Today is Pom's mom's birthday.	T	(F)
2. Pom cleared the table and loaded the dishwasher.	T	F
3. Pom bought her mom a card.	T	F
4. Pom's mom loves flowers and plants.	T	F
5. Pom will take her mom to dinner at a restaurant.	T	F
6. Pom's dad bought tickets to a show.	T	F
7. Kate is going to the supermarket.	T	F
8. Pom gives Kate her e-mail address.	T	F

C Read the sentences. Then listen to **A Special Day in Thailand** again. Complete the sentences. 🔊 18

1. Pom is tired today because it's ___Mother's Day.___

2. Pom will make her mom a special present from white _____

3. Pom did a lot of _____ in the house for her mom.

4. In the evening, Pom's dad will cook her mom a _____

D Ask and answer the questions with a partner.

1. Do you have Mother's Day in your country? If so, what do you do?

2. What holiday does your family celebrate? What do you do?

3. What is the best gift you gave someone?

4. What is the best gift someone gave you?

E Listen. Then read and choose the correct answer. 🔊 19

1. When the girl says *clear the table*, she means
   - ☐ a. put the chairs on the table.
   - ☑ b. take the things off the table.
   - ☐ c. wash the table.
   - ☐ d. put the things on the table.

2. When the boy says *mail the package*, he means
   - ☐ a. wrap a present.
   - ☐ b. send something at the post office.
   - ☐ c. open a box.
   - ☐ d. meet the postal worker.

3. When the man says *helpful*, he means
   - ☐ a. be happy.
   - ☐ b. be smart.
   - ☐ c. do things for other people.
   - ☐ d. be lazy.

4. When the woman says *water the flowers*, she means
   - ☐ a. put the flowers in the shower.
   - ☐ b. drink the flower water.
   - ☐ c. put the flowers in the rain.
   - ☐ d. pour water on the flowers.

F Look and listen. Choose the best description. 🔊 20

1.

   ☑ a. ☐ b. ☐ c. ☐ d.

2.

   ☐ a. ☐ b. ☐ c. ☐ d.

3.

   ☐ a. ☐ b. ☐ c. ☐ d.

4.

   ☐ a. ☐ b. ☐ c. ☐ d.

WHAT CAN YOU DO? Color the stars.

I can listen to a conversation and make an outline. ⭐⭐⭐

I can understand all the key words. ⭐⭐⭐

KEY
 I need help.
 I can do this a little.
 I can do this well.

Listening Check

A Listen to the story **A Visit in the Night**. What is it about? Make an outline and choose the correct answer. 🔊 21

Outline

_____

_____

_____

_____

☐ a. A fox ate Mr. Miller's seeds and plants.

☐ b. Mr. Miller's flowers and plants didn't grow because it was raining too much.

B Listen to **A Visit in the Night** again. Order the pictures. 🔊 22

a.  ☐

b.  ☐

c.  1

C Think about **A Visit in the Night**. Then choose the correct answer.

1. You want to know what happens after Mr. Miller sees the fox. What should you do?

☐ a. listen for sequence ☐ b. listen and make an outline

2. You want to know the main ideas and details of the story. What should you do?

☐ a. listen for sequence ☐ b. listen and make an outline

D Answer the questions and discuss your answers with the class.

1. What happens at the beginning of the story? What happens next? What happens at the end?

2. What heading and bullets did you use in your outline? Why?

E Listen to **A Visit in the Night** again. Choose the correct answer. 🔊 23

1. When did Mr. Miller plant the seeds?
   - ☐ a. in the summer
   - ☐ b. in the winter
   - ☐ c. in the fall
   - ☑ d. in the spring

2. What did Mr. Miller do after he took out the trash?
   - ☐ a. watered the seeds and plants
   - ☐ b. fed the cat
   - ☐ c. cleaned the patio
   - ☐ d. planted some seeds

3. What did Mr. Miller find on his patio one morning?
   - ☐ a. newspapers
   - ☐ b. a cat
   - ☐ c. old food and plastic
   - ☐ d. a package of seeds

4. What was Mr. Miller's good idea?
   - ☐ a. to feed the fox
   - ☐ b. to take out the trash in the morning
   - ☐ c. to put the flowers in the kitchen
   - ☐ d. to call the police

F Discuss with a partner.

1. Have you ever had a mystery to solve? What happened?
2. Was it a good idea for Mr. Miller to feed the fox? Why or why not?
3. How would you stop an animal or bird from eating your garden?

G Listen and read. Complete the sentences. 🔊 24

My children are very (1) _____helpful_____ at home. They
(2) _____ after meals and (3) _____.
Then they (4) _____ and put them in the cupboard.
They love to garden and help their dad (5) _____ and
flowers. They know it's important to (6) _____, too.
They don't like (7) _____ or (8) _____, so
those are my chores!

WHAT CAN YOU DO? Color the stars.

I can listen for sequence.
⭐⭐⭐

I can listen and make an outline.
⭐⭐⭐

KEY
⭐ I need help.
⭐⭐ I can do this a little.
⭐⭐⭐ I can do this well.

Get Ready to Speak

SPEAKING GOAL: Give Instructions

Instructions tell a person how to do or make something. It's important to include steps with detailed information when giving instructions to someone.

A Read and listen to the instructions. Underline the sequence words. 25

> **Speaking Tip**
> To introduce steps in your instructions, use simple sequence words and phrases like *first*, *after that*, and *finally*.

Growing Sunflowers

Peter: Hi, Mary. Those sunflowers are so tall. They look amazing. How do you grow them? I want to learn.

Mary: <u>First</u>, you plant the sunflower seeds in a small pot. Next, you put the pot in a sunny place.

Peter: OK. After that, do you need to water them every day?

Mary: Yes, that's right. Then, after a few weeks, you plant them in the garden.

Peter: Oh. I don't have a garden.

Mary: No problem. You could also put them in a big pot.

Peter: OK, great. Is that all?

Mary: Finally, you have to take care of them and remember to water them.

Peter: Sounds easy! But first I have to remember to plant the sunflower seeds and not eat them!

B Discuss the questions with a partner.

1. What do Mary's instructions teach?
2. What is the first step of her instructions?
3. What is the last step of her instructions?
4. What does Peter need to remember?

NATURAL SPEECH: Sentence Stress

You stress important words when you speak. This means you say them a little more loudly. Important words are nouns, verbs, adjectives, and adverbs.

You **plant** the **seeds** in a **small pot**. 26

Listen for stress in **A** . Then write three sentences about how to do something. Say them with stress to your partner.

Speak

C Think about something you know how to do very well. Complete the chart with your instructions.

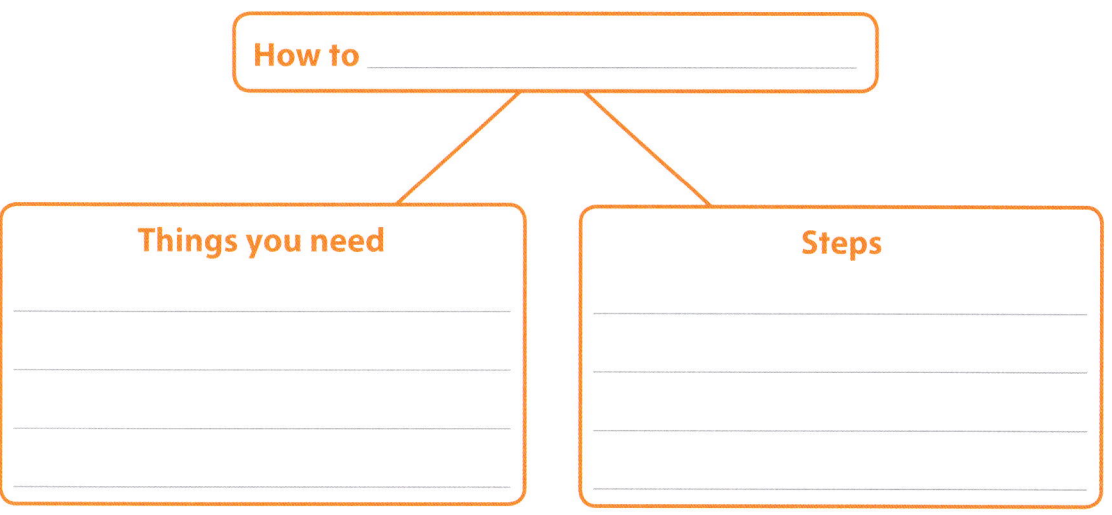

How to _____

Things you need	Steps
_____	_____
_____	_____
_____	_____
	_____

D Write your instructions. Use your words from **C**. Choose new words, too.

1. What do you want to teach someone how to do?

   _____

2. What do you need?

   _____

3. What is the first step in your instructions?

   _____

4. What are the next steps?

   _____

 Work with a partner. Tell each other how to do something. Use your instructions.

WHAT CAN YOU DO? Color the stars.

I can give instructions. ⭐⭐⭐

I can use sequence words to show the steps. ⭐⭐⭐

KEY
⭐ I need help.
⭐⭐ I can do this a little.
⭐⭐⭐ I can do this well.

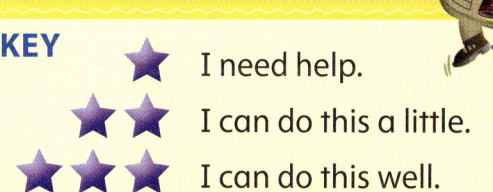

TOPIC

2

SOCIAL STUDIES

Let's Go on Vacation!

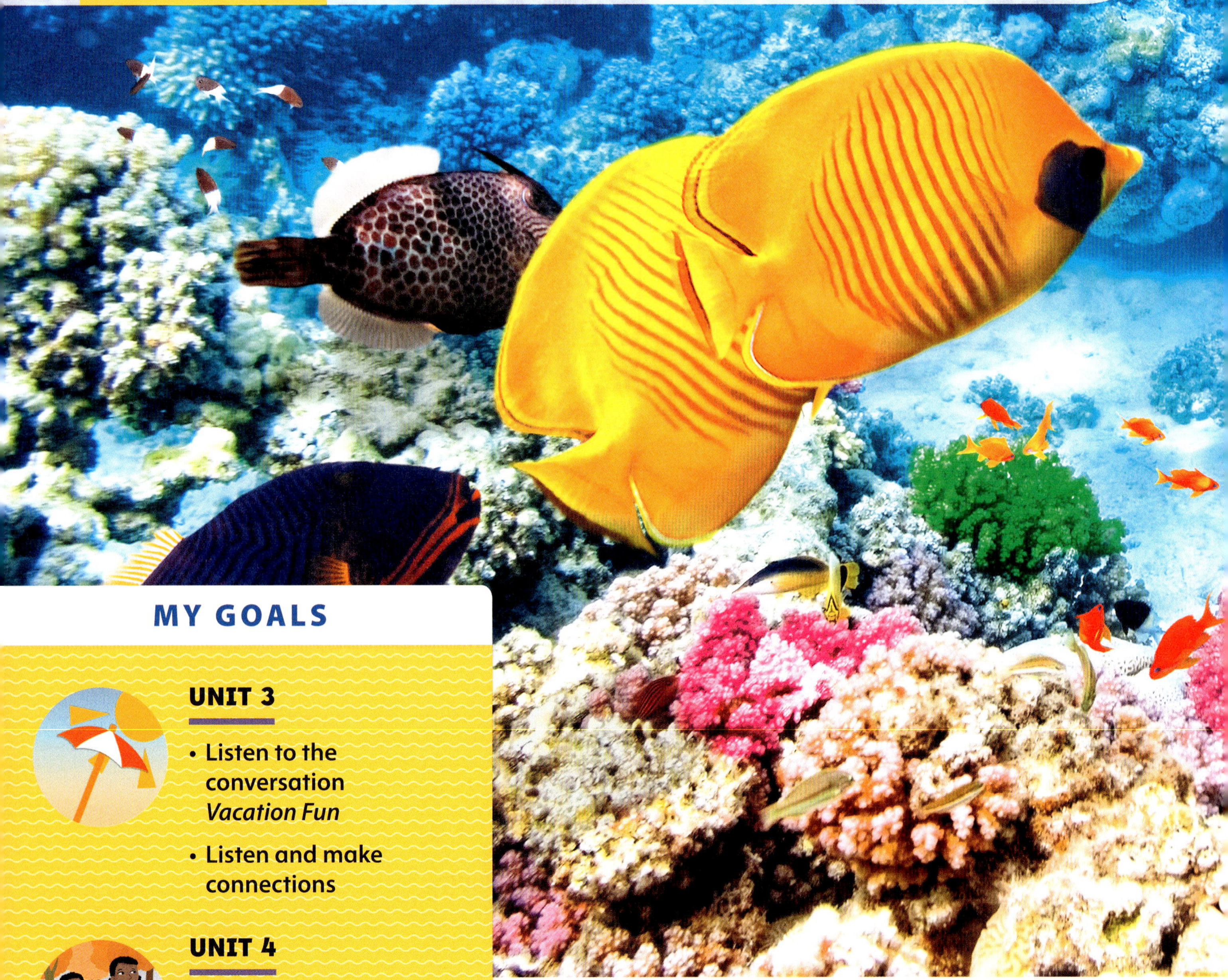

MY GOALS

UNIT 3

- Listen to the conversation *Vacation Fun*
- Listen and make connections

UNIT 4

- Listen to the story *Falling Leaves, Falling Snow*
- Listen and draw conclusions

SPEAK

- Make suggestions

A Look at the picture.

1. What do you see in the picture?
2. Have you ever been anywhere like this? Where?

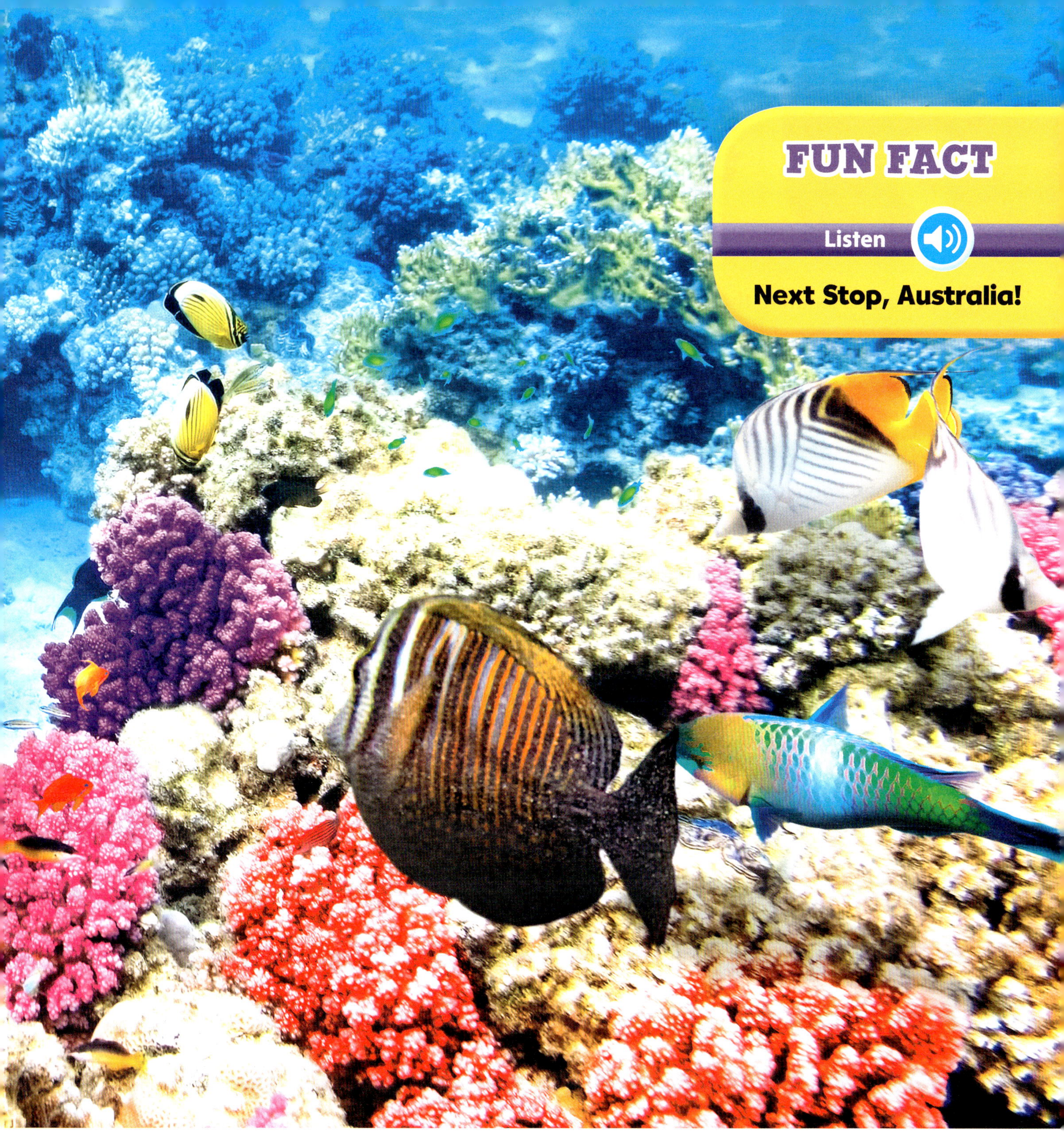

FUN FACT

Listen

Next Stop, Australia!

B **Listen to the Fun Fact. Then answer the questions.** 27

1. How many beaches does Australia have?
2. What can you see from the moon?
3. Would you like to go on a beach vacation? If so, where?

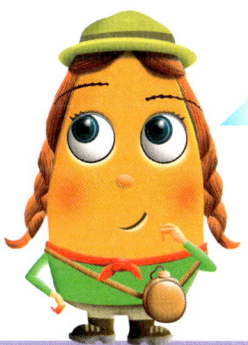

Think, Pair, Share
Where is your favorite place to go on vacation? Why?

Get Ready to Listen

Let's learn the **key words**.

A Read and listen to the sentences. Look up the words you don't know in your dictionary. 🔊 28

1. When I **make a sandcastle**, I use shells for the windows.
2. It's snowing. Let's go **make a snowman** outside.
3. My brother loves **sledding** down snowy hills.
4. When I go **snorkeling**, I see colorful fish.
5. It is easy to fall over when you are **snowboarding**.
6. The waves are great for **surfing** today.
7. We went **waterskiing** on the lake with my uncle's boat.
8. A windy day at the beach is perfect to go **windsurfing**.

B Listen and number. 🔊 29

C Listen and complete the sentences. 🔊 30

Yesterday my school was closed because it snowed all night. I met my friends in the park where the snow was perfect for (1) _____ down the hill. Later, we (2) _____ and put a hat and scarf on it. My brother loves (3) _____, so he came with us to practice. It was a fun day!

Listen

LISTENING GOAL: Listen and Make Connections

You can make connections between a listening and your own experiences. When you listen, ask *How is this similar to my life?* Your answers can give you a deeper understanding of the listening.

A Listen. Choose the answer that makes a connection. 🔊 31

1. ☐ a. In the summer, I like to go to the mountains, too.   ☐ b. In the winter, I like to go skiing, too.

2. ☐ a. I like winter sports because I love the snow, too.   ☐ b. I enjoy going to the beach, too, because I like water sports.

3. ☐ a. I enjoy learning new activities, too.   ☐ b. I don't like to try new things.

Vacation Fun

B Listen to the conversation *Vacation Fun*. What is it about? Take notes. 🔊 32

Notes

_____

_____

_____

_____

What **connections** did you make to the story?

Now put the sentences in order.

a. Kimi went to Japan. Ann went to Australia.   ☐

b. Kimi and Ann ask about each other's vacations.   ☐

c. Kimi and Ann learned how to do different activities.   ☐

WHAT CAN YOU DO?   Color the stars.

I can listen and make connections to my life.
⭐⭐⭐

I can understand all the key words.
⭐⭐⭐

KEY
⭐ I need help.
⭐⭐ I can do this a little.
⭐⭐⭐ I can do this well.

Understand

Remember!
Make **connections** with your own life and experiences when listening.

A Think about **Vacation Fun**. Make connections.
Answer the questions and discuss with the class.

1. What is the weather like in your country in December?

2. Have you tried any of the activities that Ann and Kimi did? Which ones?

3. Would you rather go to Japan or Australia? Why?

B Listen to **Vacation Fun** again. Choose the correct answer. 🔊 33

1. What was the weather like in Australia?

☐ a. It was very hot.

☐ b. It rained.

☐ c. It was cold.

☐ d. It was windy.

2. What lessons did Ann take in Australia?

☐ a. snorkeling

☐ b. waterskiing

☐ c. windsurfing

☐ d. surfing

3. What lessons did Kimi take on vacation?

☐ a. sledding

☐ b. snorkeling

☐ c. making a snowman

☐ d. snowboarding

4. What's Ann's idea?

☐ a. They go snorkeling together.

☐ b. They switch vacation countries.

☐ c. They have windsurfing lessons.

☐ d. They go on vacation together.

C Read the sentences. Then listen to **Vacation Fun** again.
Choose the correct answer. 🔊 34

1. Kimi and Ann went on a **winter** / **summer** / **fall** vacation.

2. Kimi was **making a snowman** / **sledding** / **snowboarding** while Ann was making a sandcastle.

3. Kimi thought her snowboarding lessons were **fun** / **difficult** / **cold**.

4. It was **easy** / **hard** / **interesting** for Ann to learn windsurfing.

D Ask and answer the questions with a partner.

1. What did you do on your last vacation?

2. Which country would you like to visit on your next vacation? Why?

3. Why is it good to learn how to do new things?

E Listen and complete the sentences. 🔊 35

| making a sandcastle | surfing | making a snowman | sledding |
| snorkeling | snowboarding | windsurfing | waterskiing |

1. In the summer, I'm going to go _____ at the Great Barrier Reef.
2. There's a storm coming. Sorry, no _____ today.
3. Look out behind you! He's _____
4. My hands are very cold after _____
5. You need to hold the rope very tight when you go _____
6. _____ is now a sport at the Winter Olympics.
7. Max isn't very good at _____ yet. He can't stand up.
8. My little sister wants to go _____. I'll have to pull her.

F Listen to the voice mails. Complete the phone messages. 🔊 36

While you were out Kimi called

Kimi's vacation

Activities: _____

_____

_____

While you were out Ann called

Ann's vacation

Activities: _____

_____

_____

WHAT CAN YOU DO? Color the stars.

I can listen to make connections to my own life. ⭐⭐⭐

KEY ⭐ I need help.

⭐⭐ I can do this a little.

⭐⭐⭐ I can do this well.

Get Ready to Listen

Let's learn the **key words**.

A Read and listen to the sentences. Look up the words you don't know in your dictionary. 🔊 37

1. It's so cold that there are long **icicles** hanging from the roof.
2. When we went camping, my dad **made a fire** for us to sit around.
3. The sun is shining and the snowman will **melt**.
4. If we go **pick apples**, we can make an apple pie.
5. In the fall I enjoy **raking the leaves** in the backyard.
6. My favorite **season** is summer because I love going to the beach.
7. Did you know every **snowflake** is a different shape?
8. Be careful when you **throw snowballs**. They can hurt someone.

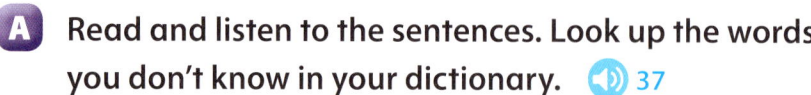

B Listen and write the number under the picture. 🔊 38

a. ____   b. ____   c. ____   d. ____

C Read each sentence. Then listen to the words. Two of the three key words are incorrect. Listen and write the correct key word. 🔊 39

1. Winter, spring, summer, and fall are all this.   _____
2. First you make snow into a ball, and then you do this.   _____
3. I enjoy doing this chore in the backyard in the fall.   _____
4. Before you make an apple pie, you need to do this.   _____

Listen

LISTENING GOAL: Listen and Draw Conclusions

You can draw conclusions about what a listening doesn't tell you. A conclusion is a guess about what happened or what may happen. Use clues in the listening passage and your own experiences to draw conclusions.

A Listen and choose a conclusion. 🔊 40

1. At home the children will probably **play in the snow / do their homework**.
2. Billy probably **fell in the snow / didn't do his homework**.
3. Mom will probably **make / buy** an apple pie for dessert.

Falling Leaves, Falling Snow

B Listen to the story *Falling Leaves, Falling Snow*. What is it about? Take notes. 🔊 41

Notes

Now read. Choose **T** for **True** or **F** for **False**.

1. The Martin family stayed on a farm.   T   F
2. The family did lots of activities.   T   F
3. The family didn't enjoy their vacation.   T   F

How do clues help you **draw conclusions**?

WHAT CAN YOU DO? Color the stars.

I can listen for clues in a story. ⭐⭐⭐
I can understand all the key words. ⭐⭐⭐

KEY
⭐ I need help.
⭐⭐ I can do this a little.
⭐⭐⭐ I can do this well.

Understand

Remember!
Use your own experiences to help you **draw conclusions**.

A Think about **Falling Leaves, Falling Snow**.
Answer the questions and discuss with the class.

1. Why does the farmer think it's going to snow?

2. How do the parents and the children feel when they see the snow?

3. Do you think the family will go to the farm again? Why or why not?

4. Can you draw conclusions about other vacations the Martin family likes? How?

B Listen to **Falling Leaves, Falling Snow** again. Choose **T** for **True** or **F** for **False**. 🔊 42

1. The Martin family went on vacation in the fall.	T	F
2. The family stayed on the beach.	T	F
3. The family didn't go hiking.	T	F
4. The family was surprised that it snowed.	T	F
5. The children were unhappy when they saw the snow.	T	F
6. Mom and Dad didn't want to play in the snow.	T	F
7. The family threw snowballs and made a snowman.	T	F
8. The family had a fun vacation.	T	F

C Read the sentences. Then listen to **Falling Leaves, Falling Snow** again. Complete the sentences. 🔊 43

1. The Martin family enjoys going on vacations in the _____

2. The family _____ the animals on the farm.

3. Mom and Dad were _____ when they saw the snow.

4. Sue thinks throwing snowballs sounds like _____

D Ask and answer the questions with a partner.

1. What is your favorite season to go on vacation? Why?

2. What do you think makes a good vacation? Why?

3. What are your favorite activities to do on vacation?

4. How do you feel when things change because of the weather?

E Listen. Then read and choose the correct answer. 🔊 44

1. When the girl says there are four *seasons*, she means
   - [ ] a. winter, spring, summer, and fall.
   - [ ] b. sun, snow, wind, and rain.
   - [ ] c. December, April, July, and November.
   - [ ] d. Children's Day, New Year's Day, Father's Day, and Mother's Day.

2. When the boy says *pick apples*, he means
   - [ ] a. to choose some apples at the store.
   - [ ] b. to choose apple juice.
   - [ ] c. to take the apples off a tree.
   - [ ] d. to give the apples to someone.

3. When the man says *raking the leaves*, he means
   - [ ] a. putting the leaves in the trash.
   - [ ] b. cleaning leaves from the ground.
   - [ ] c. playing in the leaves.
   - [ ] d. picking the leaves from the tree.

4. When the woman says the ice *melts*, she means
   - [ ] a. the ice is hard.
   - [ ] b. the ice is ice cream.
   - [ ] c. the ice changes to water.
   - [ ] d. the ice is very cold.

F Look and listen. Choose the best description. 🔊 45

1.
   [ ] a. [ ] b. [ ] c. [ ] d.

2.
   [ ] a. [ ] b. [ ] c. [ ] d.

3.
   [ ] a. [ ] b. [ ] c. [ ] d.

4.
   [ ] a. [ ] b. [ ] c. [ ] d.

WHAT CAN YOU DO? Color the stars.

I can listen for clues in a story to draw conclusions. ⭐⭐⭐

I can understand all the key words. ⭐⭐⭐

KEY
⭐ I need help.
⭐⭐ I can do this a little.
⭐⭐⭐ I can do this well.

Listening Check

Remember!
Listen for **connections** to your experiences and clues to help you **draw conclusions**.

A Listen to the presentation **From Beaches to Mountains**. What is it about? Take notes and choose the correct answer. 🔊 46

Notes

_____

_____

_____

_____

☐ a. a family vacation in Chile

☐ b. dangerous sports

B Listen to **From Beaches to Mountains** again. Order the pictures. 🔊 47

a. ☐   b. ☐   c. ☐

C Think about **From Beaches to Mountains**. Then choose the correct answer.

1. You want to know which activities the family likes to do. What should you do?

☐ a. listen and draw a conclusion   ☐ b. listen and make connections

2. You want to see how similar the vacation is to one of yours. What should you do?

☐ a. listen and draw a conclusion   ☐ b. listen and make connections

D Answer the questions and discuss your answers with the class.

1. Have you ever had a vacation like this? What was similar and what was different?

2. What conclusions can you draw about the family's vacation?

E Listen to **From Beaches to Mountains** again. Choose the correct answer. 🔊 48

1. Where did the family go on vacation?
   - ☐ a. Italy
   - ☐ b. Chile
   - ☐ c. Japan
   - ☐ d. Australia

2. What did Tim see on the last day?
   - ☐ a. a shark
   - ☐ b. snow
   - ☐ c. snowballs
   - ☐ d. a sandcastle

3. What did the family do after their trip to the mountains?
   - ☐ a. they went home
   - ☐ b. they visited friends
   - ☐ c. they went back to the beach
   - ☐ d. they watched a soccer game

4. What did the family do around the fire?
   - ☐ a. played a guessing game
   - ☐ b. sang songs
   - ☐ c. made a sand castle
   - ☐ d. told family stories

F Discuss with a partner.

1. How does your family decide where to go on vacation?

2. What did you learn on your last vacation?

3. What family activities does your family like to do on vacation?

G Listen and read. Complete the sentences. 🔊 49

Looking for a family vacation at the beach or in the mountains? Want to take (1) _____ or (2) _____ classes, or go (3) _____ in clear waters? Then try the beaches of South Africa! Or how about (4) _____, (5) _____ down the hills, and (6) _____? Then you should plan your next trip to France before the snow (7) _____. Call us now about our winter (8) _____ prices.

WHAT CAN YOU DO? Color the stars.

I can listen and make connections to my own life. ⭐⭐⭐

I can listen for clues to help me draw conclusions. ⭐⭐⭐

KEY
⭐ I need help.
⭐⭐ I can do this a little.
⭐⭐⭐ I can do this well.

Get Ready to Speak

SPEAKING GOAL: Make Suggestions

We make suggestions to give an idea or a plan for someone to think about.

A Read and listen to the conversation. Underline the suggestion phrases. 50

> **Speaking Tip**
> Use *Let's*, *How about*, *What about*, and *Why don't* to make suggestions.

Where Should We Go?

Dad: Where do you want to go on our next vacation?

Mom: How about the mountains?

Penny: It's cold in the mountains. Why don't we go somewhere sunny? I'd like a quiet beach where we can relax and do some water sports.

Mom: I want to do more than relax! What about a forest? The mountains are close for hiking, but it's warmer.

Penny: I'd love to go camping in the forest! We could hike in the mountains and go waterskiing on a lake.

Dad: OK! Let's look for somewhere that is in a forest, that is close to the mountains, and that has a lake or a beach with lots of activities to do.

Mom: Why don't we go to Hawaii?

Dad: Great idea. When do you want to go?

Penny: How about tomorrow?

B Discuss the questions with a partner.

1. What kind of vacation does Penny want?
2. Where does Mom want to go?
3. Why is the forest a good suggestion for a place to go?
4. Where do Dad, Mom, and Penny finally decide to go on vacation?

NATURAL SPEECH: *Want To*

Want to is a phrase with connected words that are often said together when you speak quickly.

Where do you **wanna** go?

I **wanna** go to the park. 🔊 51

Listen for the connected words in **A**. Then write three sentences about a vacation using the connected words. Say them with your partner.

Speak

C Think about where you want to go on vacation. What do you want to do there? Complete the diagram with your ideas.

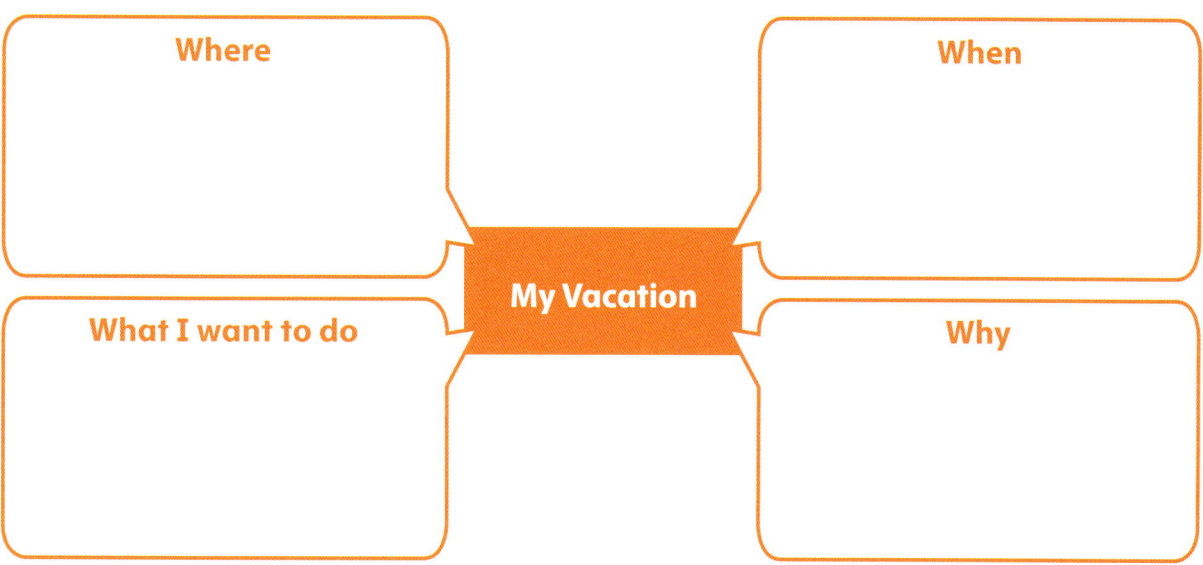

D Write about your vacation. Use your words from **C**. Choose new words, too.

1. Where do you want to go?

_____

2. Why do you want to go there?

_____

3. What do you want to do?

_____

4. When do you want to go?

_____

 Talk to your partner about your vacation ideas. Make suggestions and agree on an idea.

WHAT CAN YOU DO?   Color the stars.

I can make suggestions. ★★★

I can use suggestion phrases. ★★★

KEY

★ I need help.

★★ I can do this a little.

★★★ I can do this well.

TOPIC

3

SCIENCE

Food, Wonderful Food!

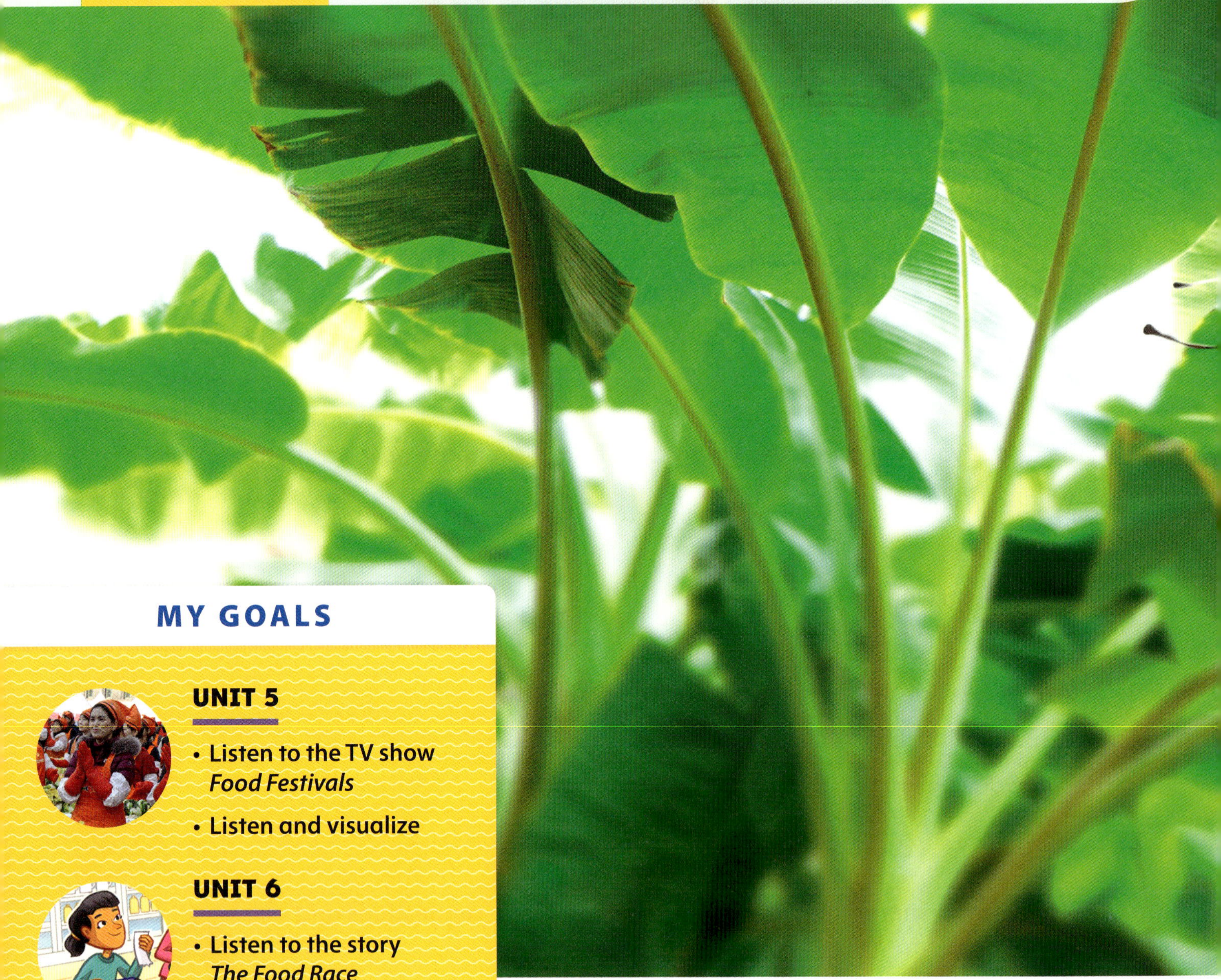

MY GOALS

UNIT 5

- Listen to the TV show *Food Festivals*
- Listen and visualize

UNIT 6

- Listen to the story *The Food Race*
- Listen to classify and categorize

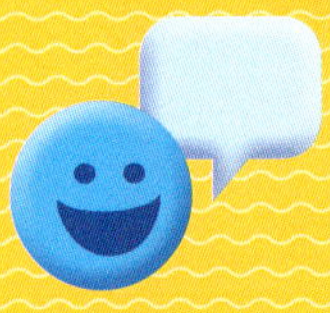

SPEAK

- Give a group presentation

A Look at the picture.

1. What fruit do you see? What can you make with it?
2. Where do you think this fruit grows?

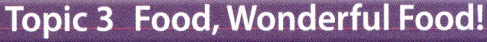

B Listen to the Fun Fact. Then answer the questions. 🔊 52

1. What country started making clothes from the banana plant in the 1300s?

2. What other things do people make from banana plants?

3. Would you wear clothes made from banana plants? Why or why not?

Think, Pair, Share
What fruits grow in your country? Which is your favorite? Why?

Get Ready to Listen

Let's learn the **key words**.

A Read and listen to the sentences. Look up the words you don't know in your dictionary. 🔊 53

1. **Exotic fruits** come from faraway countries.
2. **Garlic** is a plant used to make food taste delicious.
3. **Kimchi** is a Korean dish made with cabbage.
4. A **kiwi** is a small, green, and sweet fruit.
5. A **papaya** is an orange fruit with black seeds inside.
6. **Red peppers** are vegetables. They make a colorful salad.
7. There are a lot of different **spices** in Asian food.
8. A **watermelon** is a big, round, and green fruit. It's red on the inside.

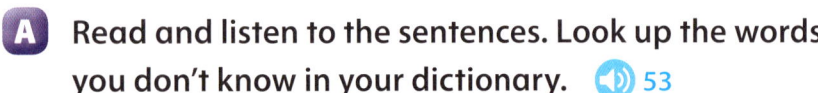

B Listen and number. 🔊 54

C Listen and complete the sentences. 🔊 55

Min-Ho, my friend from Korea, loves (1) _____. He eats it every day. He has it with breakfast, lunch, and dinner! His mom made it for me last week. I liked the cabbage with the (2) _____ and other (3) _____. It was very tasty. Tomorrow, my mom's going to make him my favorite food. It's chicken with (4) _____ on rice.

Listen

LISTENING GOAL: Listen and Visualize

Speakers use words to help you visualize, or create pictures in your mind. When you listen, notice the words the speaker uses to describe people, places, or things. Try to see them in your mind.

A Listen. Which words help you visualize a picture? Choose the correct answer. 🔊 56

1. ☐ a. strange ☐ b. red with lots of hair
2. ☐ a. busy and colorful ☐ b. vegetable
3. ☐ a. fruit ☐ b. looks like a green football

Food Festivals

B Listen to the TV show *Food Festivals*. What is it about? Take notes. 🔊 57

Notes

Now put the events in order.

a. Mark says everyone should visit Asia. ☐

b. Mark talks about another festival in Thailand. ☐

c. Mark went to a food festival in South Korea. ☐

What kind of words and phrases help you **visualize** a story?

WHAT CAN YOU DO? Color the stars.

I can notice the words a speaker uses to describe things and visualize them. ⭐⭐⭐

I can understand all the key words. ⭐⭐⭐

KEY

⭐ I need help.

⭐⭐ I can do this a little.

⭐⭐⭐ I can do this well.

Understand

A Think about **Food Festivals**. What words help you visualize? Answer the questions and discuss with the class.

1. How many types of kimchi are there at the festival?

2. What colors are the fruits and vegetables in Thailand?

3. What are the kiwis like?

B Listen to **Food Festivals** again. Choose the correct answer. 🔊 58

1. Where does Mark go to visit food festivals?

   ☐ a. Asia

   ☐ b. South America

   ☐ c. the US

   ☐ d. Europe

2. What is in kimchi?

   ☐ a. tomato

   ☐ b. cabbage and garlic

   ☐ c. salad

   ☐ d. rice

3. What does Mark hear at the kimchi race?

   ☐ a. people cutting red peppers

   ☐ b. people cheering

   ☐ c. people running fast

   ☐ d. people cutting cabbage

4. What fruit did Mark see in Thailand?

   ☐ a. bananas

   ☐ b. oranges

   ☐ c. watermelons

   ☐ d. apples

C Read the sentences. Then listen to **Food Festivals** again. Choose the correct answer. 🔊 59

1. There is a kimchi **race** / **video** / **talk** at the festival.

2. Mark likes the **salty** / **sweet** / **sour** taste of kimchi.

3. The papayas look **shiny** / **nice** / **soft** in the warm sun.

4. The festival in Thailand was very **hot** / **interesting** / **colorful**.

D Ask and answer the questions with a partner.

1. Which food festival would you like to go to?

2. Does your country have a famous food festival?

3. Are there other famous festivals in your country?

4. What type of festival would you like to go to?

Listen and complete the sentences. 🔊 60

kiwi	watermelon	red peppers	papaya
kimchi	spices	garlic	exotic fruits

1. Tim tried _____ when he was on vacation last year.

2. _____ salad is my favorite dish.

3. In the supermarket, there are a few _____

4. _____ is from China.

5. At the market, the _____ are all different colors.

6. My mom is growing _____ in our garden.

7. Chicken with _____ is delicious.

8. I love eating _____ in the summer.

F **Listen to Max plan a meal. Fill in the information.** 🔊 61

Fried noodles

tomatoes

(1) _____

chicken

(2) _____

cabbage

(3) _____

(4) _____

Fruit salad

mango

(5) _____

(6) _____

(7) _____

WHAT CAN YOU DO? Color the stars.

I can listen and create a picture in my mind. ⭐⭐⭐

I can understand all the key words. ⭐⭐⭐

KEY ⭐ I need help.

⭐⭐ I can do this a little.

⭐⭐⭐ I can do this well.

Get Ready to Listen

Let's learn the **key words**.

A Read and listen to the sentences. Look up the words you don't know in your dictionary 🔊 62

1. My mom uses a **can of tomatoes** to make spaghetti sauce.

2. Is the **carton of juice** in the refrigerator orange or apple juice?

3. How many **chili peppers** did you put in the soup? It's really spicy!

4. I love a little bit of **cinnamon** and sugar on top of my donuts.

5. Max likes to make his tea sweet with **honey**.

6. Can you cut some green **melon** to put in the fruit salad, please?

7. The dark green **spinach** makes my salad healthy and colorful.

8. **Yogurt** is a healthier dessert than ice cream.

B Listen and write the number under the picture. 🔊 63

a. _____

b. _____

c. _____

d. _____

C Read each sentence. Then listen to the words. Two of the three key words are incorrect. Write the correct key word. 🔊 64

1. You have to open this before you can eat it. _____

2. This fruit is usually round and sweet. _____

3. This is delicious on pancakes. _____

4. It's a green vegetable you can cook or eat in a salad. _____

Listen

LISTENING GOAL: Listen to Classify and Categorize

When you listen, you can classify and categorize to understand how things are similar and different. To classify, put similar things into a group. To categorize, give the group a name that describes it.

A Listen. Then classify and categorize. 🔊 65

Fruits I Like	Vegetables I Like	4. _____
bananas	2. _____	tea
1. _____	3. _____	5. _____

🛒 The Food Race

B Listen to the story *The Food Race*. What is it about? Take notes. 🔊 66

Notes

_____

_____

_____

_____

_____

Now read. Choose **T** for **True** or **F** for **False**.

1. The story is outside.   T   F
2. Patty and Max play a shopping game.   T   F
3. Max wins the race.   T   F

How do **classifying** and **categorizing** help you understand similarities and differences?

WHAT CAN YOU DO?   Color the stars.

I can listen to classify and categorize things.
⭐⭐⭐

I can understand all the key words.
⭐⭐⭐

KEY

⭐ I need help.

⭐⭐ I can do this a little.

⭐⭐⭐ I can do this well.

Understand

A Think about **The Food Race**. Answer the questions and discuss with the class.

1. What things on Max's and Patty's lists are similar?

2. What cold things do Patty and Max need to find?

3. How would you categorize the things they bought?

B Listen to **The Food Race** again. Choose **T** for **True** or **F** for **False**. 🔊 67

1. Patty had spinach and a carton of juice on her list.	T	F
2. Max had yogurt and honey on his list.	T	F
3. Mom didn't have anything to get.	T	F
4. Patty made a good plan.	T	F
5. Max ran around the store with no plan.	T	F
6. Max didn't get everything on his list.	T	F
7. Mom thanked the children for helping her.	T	F
8. Mom gave Max and Patty chocolate.	T	F

C Read the sentences. Then listen to **The Food Race** again. Complete the sentences. 🔊 68

1. To make shopping more fun, Mom thought of a _____

2. Patty found the _____ things on her list first.

3. Max didn't have a _____ for the shopping race.

4. Max arrived _____ after Patty.

D Ask and answer the questions with a partner.

1. How did Patty's plan help her win the race?

2. How can categorizing and classifying things help you shop?

3. Do you enjoy shopping with your parents? Why or why not?

4. Would you enjoy shopping if you played a game like this? Why or why not?

E Listen. Then read and choose the correct answer. 🔊 69

1. When the girl says *honey*, she means
   - ☐ a. a fruit.
   - ☐ b. a sweet, sticky food.
   - ☐ c. a vegetable.
   - ☐ d. a type of yogurt.

2. When the boy says *yogurt*, he means
   - ☐ a. a white food made from milk.
   - ☐ b. ice cream with fruit.
   - ☐ c. a carton of fruit juice.
   - ☐ d. a glass of soda.

3. When the man says *spinach*, he means
   - ☐ a. an orange vegetable.
   - ☐ b. a round, red vegetable.
   - ☐ c. a long, green vegetable.
   - ☐ d. a green vegetable with leaves.

4. When the woman says *melon*, she means
   - ☐ a. a small, hairy fruit.
   - ☐ b. a round or oval fruit that is sweet.
   - ☐ c. a green vegetable with leaves.
   - ☐ d. a long yellow fruit.

F Look and listen. Choose the best description. 🔊 70

1.
☐ a. ☐ b. ☐ c. ☐ d.

2.
☐ a. ☐ b. ☐ c. ☐ d.

3.
☐ a. ☐ b. ☐ c. ☐ d.

4.
☐ a. ☐ b. ☐ c. ☐ d.

WHAT CAN YOU DO? Color the stars.

I can listen for how similar things are classified and categorized.
⭐⭐⭐

KEY
⭐ I need help.
⭐⭐ I can do this a little.
⭐⭐⭐ I can do this well.

Listening Check

A Listen to the TV show **Food Art**. What is it about? Take notes and choose the correct answer. 🔊 71

Notes

_____

_____

_____

_____

☐ a. fruit and vegetable markets around the world

☐ b. an art contest

B Listen to **Food Art** again. Order the pictures. 🔊 72

a. FOOD ART CONTEST
THE ART of FOOD
☐

b. ☐

c. ☐

C Think about **Food Art**. Then choose the correct answer.

1. You want to know what the food looks like. What should you do?

   ☐ a. listen and visualize   ☐ b. classify and categorize

2. You want to find out what kind of food made the art. What should you do?

   ☐ a. listen and visualize   ☐ b. classify and categorize

D Answer the questions and discuss your answers with the class.

1. What foods do you think would make good food art?

2. Have you been in a contest? If so, what was it for?

E Listen to **Food Art** again. Choose the correct answer. 🔊 73

1. What does Sally make?
   - [ ] a. a frog
   - [ ] b. a fish
   - [ ] c. a dog
   - [ ] d. a cat

2. What does Omar make?
   - [ ] a. a monkey
   - [ ] b. a scary head
   - [ ] c. a book
   - [ ] d. a flying bird

3. What does Sally use for the eyes?
   - [ ] a. grapes
   - [ ] b. tomatoes
   - [ ] c. lemons
   - [ ] d. garlic

4. What does Omar use for the teeth?
   - [ ] a. kiwis
   - [ ] b. lemons
   - [ ] c. chili peppers
   - [ ] d. garlic

F Discuss with a partner.

1. Would you like to learn how to make food art? Why or why not?
2. What would you make in a food art contest? How?
3. How do you feel when you win a contest?

G Listen and read. Complete the sentences. 🔊 74

Mary will cook for her mom and dad later. She needs to check what food she has in the kitchen. She has some (1) _____ and (2) _____. In the garden there's some (3) _____, but there aren't any (4) _____. There's a big (5) _____ on the tree, too. She'll have to buy a (6) _____, a (7) _____, and some (8) _____ at the store.

Shopping list

WHAT CAN YOU DO? Color the stars.

I can listen and visualize. ⭐⭐⭐

I can listen to classify and categorize things. ⭐⭐⭐

KEY

⭐ I need help.

⭐⭐ I can do this a little.

⭐⭐⭐ I can do this well.

Get Ready to Speak

SPEAKING GOAL: Give a Group Presentation

A group presentation is a presentation given by more than one speaker. The group has one topic and speakers take turns talking about different ideas about the topic.

A Read and listen to the group presentation. Underline the transition phrases. 75

Speaking Tip
Use transition phrases with your group members' names to change from one speaker to the next.

We Know Our Pizza

Peter: How much do you know about pizzas? Well, they are from Italy and were first made in the 1800s. Italian people sold the first pizzas in the streets. People ate them for breakfast, lunch, and dinner. The sellers cut pieces from a large pizza. Now here is Sue to tell you more.

Sue: Thank you, Peter. The toppings were simple, like mushrooms, onions, and tomatoes. Now people put meat on their pizza, too. Mark, what can you tell us about pizzas around the world?

Mark: Thank you, Sue. Different countries have their own favorite pizza toppings. For example, in Russia they love fish, and in Sweden they love peanuts, bananas, and pineapple on their pizzas! Finally, here's Peter again to finish.

Peter: Thank you, Mark and Sue. In conclusion, people have been eating pizza for a long time. Around the world people enjoy different toppings. Thank you for listening to our presentation about pizza.

B Discuss the questions with a partner.

1. What is the topic of the presentation?
2. What idea does each presenter talk about?
3. What does each presenter say to the speaker before them?
4. What words does Peter use to end the presentation?

NATURAL SPEECH: Items in a Series

Rising intonation means your voice goes up. *Falling intonation* means your voice goes down. Use rising intonation when you say a list of items. On the last item, use falling intonation.

Toppings were simple, like mushrooms, onions, and tomatoes. 76

Listen for intonation in **A**. Then write three lists of food items. Say them, with intonation, to your partner.

Speak

C Think about a food topic for your group presentation. Fill in the chart to plan your presentation.

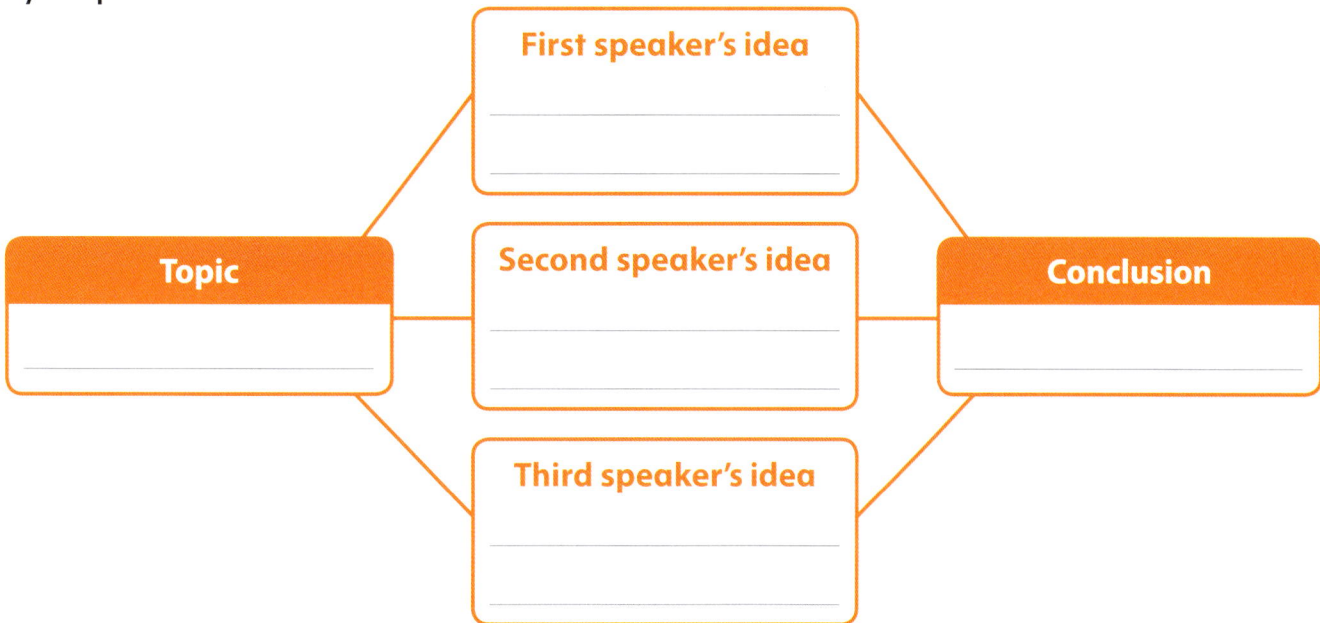

| Topic | First speaker's idea | Second speaker's idea | Third speaker's idea | Conclusion |

D Write about your presentation. Use your words from **C**. Choose new words, too.

1. What is the topic of your group's presentation?

   _____

2. What are the three ideas of your presentation?

   _____

3. What transition phrases will you use to change speakers?

   _____

4. How are you going to finish the presentation?

   _____

 Give your group presentation to another group.
Listen to the other group's presentation.

WHAT CAN YOU DO? Color the stars.

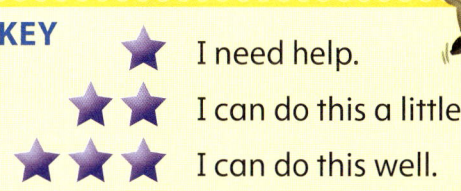

I can give a group presentation. ⭐⭐⭐

I can use transition phrases. ⭐⭐⭐

KEY
⭐ I need help.
⭐⭐ I can do this a little.
⭐⭐⭐ I can do this well.

Animal Planet

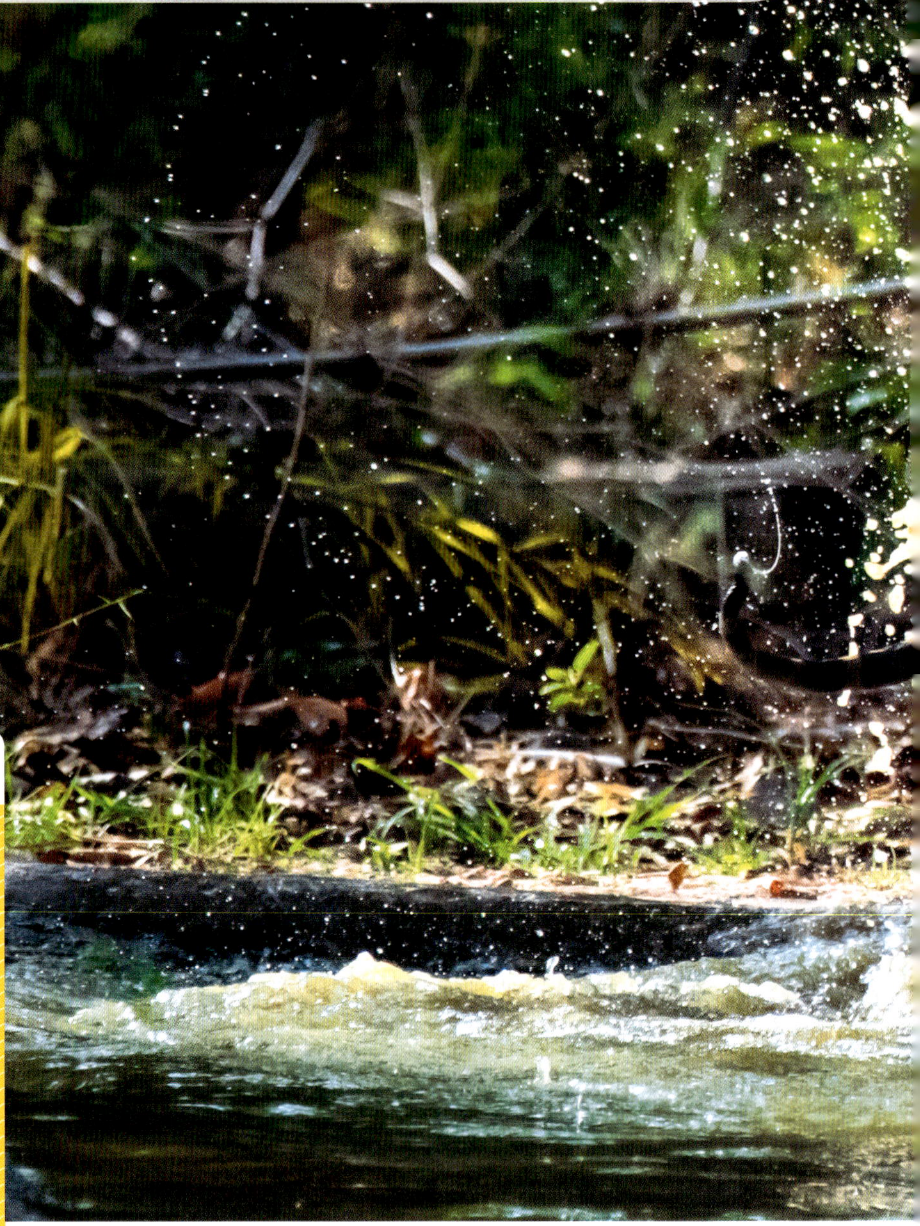

MY GOALS

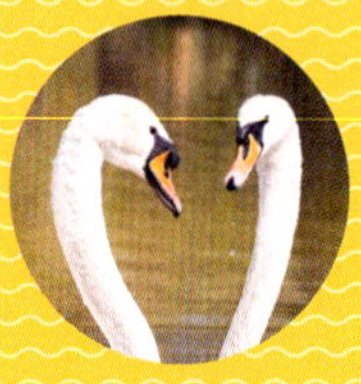

UNIT 7

- Listen to the passage *Beautiful Birds*
- Listen for opinions

UNIT 8

- Listen to the story *A Day at the Zoo*
- Listen for attitudes

SPEAK

- Persuade

A Look at the picture.

1. Where do you think these tigers are?
2. How does it make you feel when you look at the photo? Why?

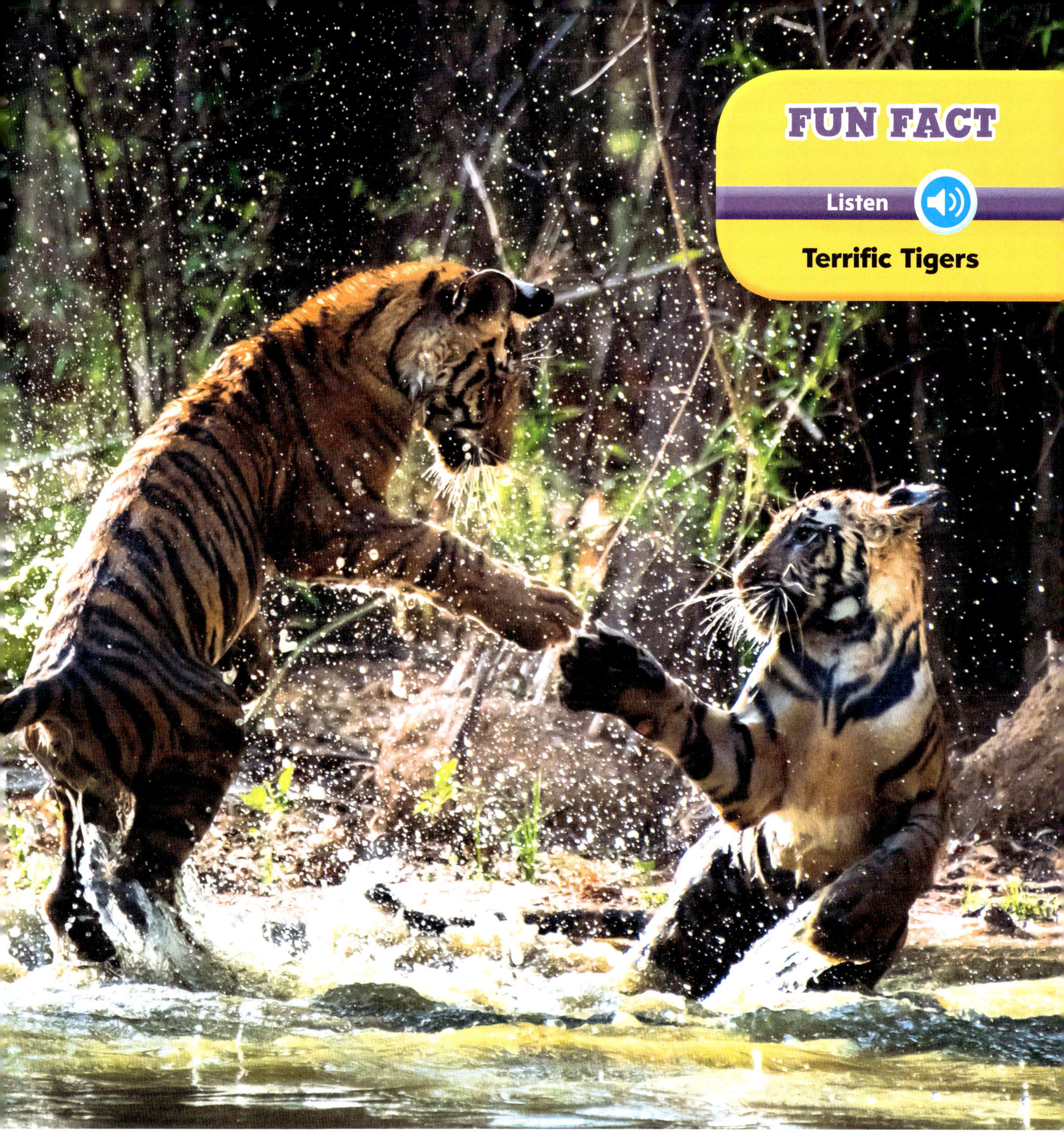

FUN FACT

Listen

Terrific Tigers

B Listen to the Fun Fact. Then answer the questions. 77

1. How high can a tiger jump?
2. How fast can a tiger run?
3. What other fast animals do you know?

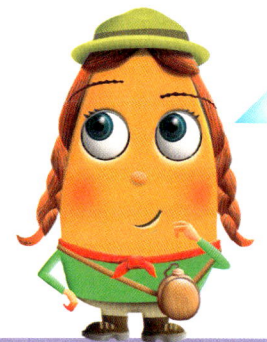

Think, Pair, Share
Which animal do you know a lot of facts about? What do you know about that animal?

Get Ready to Listen

Let's learn the **key words**.

A Read and listen to the sentences. Look up the words you don't know in your dictionary. 🔊 78

1. A **beak** is what a bird uses to eat.

2. **Eagles** are very strong birds with white heads.

3. I heard a tiger **escaped** from the zoo. I hope they catch it soon.

4. **Feathers** help birds fly and keep warm.

5. A **flamingo** is a pink bird that has very long legs and a long neck.

6. You can't always see a small **hummingbird**, but you can hear it.

7. A **peacock** has a colorful tail that looks like a fan!

8. Jenny enjoys watching the calm **swans** on the lake.

B Listen and write the number under the picture. 🔊 79

a. _____   b. _____   c. _____   d. _____

C Read each sentence. Then listen to the words. Two of the three key words are incorrect. Write the correct key word. 🔊 80

1. When you do this, you try to get away from someone or something.   _____

2. This large bird can fly very high and still see the fish below.   _____

3. This very small bird makes a *hmm* sound when it flies.   _____

4. This bird is usually white or black and you can see it on lakes.   _____

Listen

LISTENING GOAL: Listen for Opinions

An opinion is what a person thinks and feels about something. It is not a fact and not true for everyone. For example, *Peacocks are the most beautiful birds* is an opinion. Listen for opinions to know what people think about something.

A Listen and choose the correct answer. 🔊 81

1. ☐ a. fact   ☐ b. opinion
2. ☐ a. fact   ☐ b. opinion
3. ☐ a. fact   ☐ b. opinion

BEAUTIFUL BIRDS

B Listen to the passage *Beautiful Birds*. What is it about? Take notes. 🔊 82

Notes

Now read. Choose **T** for **True** or **F** for **False**.

1. The talk is at a bird zoo.   T   F
2. The man is telling the children about the birds.   T   F
3. There are only flamingos at the bird zoo.   T   F

Why is it important to know someone's **opinion**?

WHAT CAN YOU DO?   Color the stars.

I can listen and identify opinions. ★★★

I can understand all the key words. ★★★

KEY
★ I need help.
★★ I can do this a little.
★★★ I can do this well.

Understand

A Think about **Beautiful Birds**. Answer the questions and discuss with the class.

1. What is the man's opinion of flamingos?

2. What facts does the man give about the eagles?

3. What is the boy's opinion about the zoo? Why?

4. What is your opinion of the zoo?

B Listen to **Beautiful Birds** again. Choose **T** for **True** or **F** for **False**. 🔊 83

1. Flamingos stand on one leg.	T	F
2. Peacocks are black and white.	T	F
3. Swans like to be alone.	T	F
4. Eagles can't see very well.	T	F
5. The name *hummingbird* comes from the noise their wings make.	T	F
6. A hummingbird is very big.	T	F
7. The birds escape from the zoo to look for food.	T	F
8. One of the children is scared of birds.	T	F

C Read each sentence. Then listen to **Beautiful Birds** again. Complete the sentences. 🔊 84

1. Flamingos like to walk in the _____

2. Peacocks have _____ on their tails.

3. Swans are sometimes _____, so don't go too close.

4. The birds don't escape because they have good _____ at the zoo.

D Ask and answer the questions with a partner.

1. Which birds are the most interesting? Why?

2. Which bird at Flying Friends Zoo would you like to see? Why?

3. How would you feel if an eagle flew close to you?

E Listen. Then read and choose the correct answer. 🔊 85

1. When the girl says the animals don't *escape*, she means
   - ☐ a. they don't play at the zoo.
   - ☐ b. they don't run away from the zoo.
   - ☐ c. they don't hurt visitors.
   - ☐ d. they don't sleep.

2. When the boy says *beak*, he means
   - ☐ a. a hard mouth.
   - ☐ b. a big foot.
   - ☐ c. a white head.
   - ☐ d. a long wing.

3. When the man says *swans*, he means
   - ☐ a. colorful birds.
   - ☐ b. large birds that swim.
   - ☐ c. birds that live in the forest.
   - ☐ d. birds that can't fly.

4. When the woman says *hummingbird*, she means
   - ☐ a. a bird that swims very fast.
   - ☐ b. the noise all birds make.
   - ☐ c. a very small bird that flies fast.
   - ☐ d. a bird that wakes up at night.

F Look and listen. Choose the best description. 🔊 86

1.
☐ a. ☐ b. ☐ c. ☐ d.

2.
☐ a. ☐ b. ☐ c. ☐ d.

3.
☐ a. ☐ b. ☐ c. ☐ d.

4.
☐ a. ☐ b. ☐ c. ☐ d.

WHAT CAN YOU DO? Color the stars.

I can listen for opinions to understand what people think about something. ★★★

KEY
★ I need help.
★★ I can do this a little.
★★★ I can do this well.

Get Ready to Listen

Let's learn the **key words**.

A Read and listen to the sentences. Look up the words you don't know in your dictionary. 🔊 87

1. Tigers are **endangered**. There aren't many alive.
2. **Gorillas** are large black animals that live in the rainforest.
3. It's better to see animals **in the wild** than in a zoo.
4. **Pandas** are black-and-white bears from China.
5. A panda's **paws** help it climb, run, and stay cool.
6. A **penguin** is a bird that can swim really fast under the ice.
7. A **rhinoceros** is a very heavy animal, and it only eats plants.
8. I want to have **wings** so I can fly like a bird.

B Listen and number. 🔊 88

ANIMALS AROUND THE WORLD

C Listen and complete the sentences. 🔊 89

In science class, Emma learned about animals (1) _____.
(2) _____, for example, eat eight hours a day. Emma also learned
that some animals are (3) _____ and need our help. In Antarctica,
(4) _____ may become endangered because the ice is melting.

Listen

LISTENING GOAL: Listen for Attitudes

An attitude is how a person feels about something. People show attitudes by their actions. They also show attitudes by their tone or how they talk. For example, an excited person talks loudly and fast. Listen for attitudes to understand how people feel.

A Listen. How do the people feel? Choose the correct answer. 🔊 90

1. ☐ a. excited
   ☐ b. bored

2. ☐ a. scared
   ☐ b. interested

3. ☐ a. surprised
   ☐ b. excited

A Day at the Zoo

B Listen to the story *A Day at the Zoo*. What is it about? Take notes. 🔊 91

Notes

_____

_____

_____

_____

_____

_____

_____

How does listening for **attitudes** help you understand a story better?

Now put the sentences in order.

a. Emma and Zac go to see the pandas. ☐

b. Emma and Zac learn it is the zookeeper's first day. ☐

c. The zookeeper answers questions about the penguins. ☐

WHAT CAN YOU DO? Color the stars.

I can listen for people's attitudes to understand how they feel. ★★★

I can understand all the key words. ★★★

KEY
★ I need help.
★★ I can do this a little.
★★★ I can do this well.

Understand

Remember!
An **attitude** is how a person feels. People show attitudes by their actions and tone.

A Think about **A Day at the Zoo**. Answer the questions and discuss with the class.

1. How does Emma feel about pandas?

2. What is Emma's attitude toward the zookeeper?

3. How do you think the zookeeper feels? How do you know?

B Listen to **A Day at the Zoo** again. Choose the correct answer. 🔊 92

1. What is as big as Emma's head?
   - ☐ a. the panda's eyes
   - ☐ b. the panda's paws
   - ☐ c. the panda's head
   - ☐ d. the panda's feet

2. Which animal does Emma say is endangered?
   - ☐ a. the giraffe
   - ☐ b. the panda
   - ☐ c. the penguin
   - ☐ d. the gorilla

3. What does Zac think is funny about the penguins?
   - ☐ a. the way they walk
   - ☐ b. the way they eat
   - ☐ c. the way they swim
   - ☐ d. the way they run

4. Why are penguins black and white?
   - ☐ a. to look like a rock
   - ☐ b. to find each other
   - ☐ c. to stay safe in the wild
   - ☐ d. to swim faster

C Read the sentences. Then listen to **A Day at the Zoo** again. Choose the correct answer. 🔊 93

1. Pandas are not **endangered** / **striped** / **interesting**.

2. The way **rhinoceroses** / **penguins** / **gorillas** walk is funny.

3. Emma is **worried** / **surprised** / **interested** by the zookeeper's answers.

4. It's the zookeeper's **first day** / **last day** / **best day** at the zoo.

D Ask and answer the questions with a partner.

1. Do you think zoos are a good idea? Why or why not?

2. What information can you learn about animals at the zoo?

3. What animal do you wish you could see in the wild?

E Listen and complete the sentences.  94

> pandas   endangered   penguin   in the wild
>
> gorillas   rhinoceroses   wings   paws

1. I watched a nature show on TV about _____

2. Mateo saw a giraffe _____ while on vacation in Africa.

3. Look, the bear is waving with his _____

4. _____ don't eat meat. They only eat plants.

5. Anna takes care of the _____ at the zoo.

6. The smallest _____ is only as long as a ruler!

7. _____ are different shapes and sizes.

8. At the zoo we learned which animals are _____

F Listen to the advertisement. Fill in the missing information. 95

I want to help with (1) _____
and exotic animals!

I want to work with:

☐ (2) _____ in Africa

☐ (3) _____ in the rainforest

☐ (4) _____ in China

☐ (5) _____ Antarctica

Please send me a panda
(6) _____ **print!**

HELP
PROTECT

WHAT CAN YOU DO? Color the stars.

I can listen to understand the
attitude of the speaker. ★ ★ ★

KEY
★ I need help.
★ ★ I can do this a little.
★ ★ ★ I can do this well.

Listening Check

Remember!
When you listen for **opinions** and **attitudes** you can understand what a person thinks and feels about something.

A Listen to the podcast **An Indian Adventure**. What's it about?
Take notes and choose the correct answer. 🔊 96

Notes

_____

_____

_____

_____

☐ a. a day at the zoo
☐ b. a day on a safari

B Listen to **An Indian Adventure** again. Order the pictures. 🔊 97

a. ☐   b. ☐   c. ☐

C Think about **An Indian Adventure**. Then choose the correct answer.

1. You want to know what Jordan thinks about animals in the wild. What do you do?

   ☐ a. listen for his opinion   ☐ b. listen for his attitude

2. You want to know how Jordan felt when the rhinoceros ran after the car. What do you do?

   ☐ a. listen for his opinion   ☐ b. listen for his attitude

D Answer the questions and discuss your answers with the class.

1. Why do you think some animals are endangered?

2. How would you feel if you saw a tiger in the wild?

Listen to An Indian Adventure again. Choose the correct answer. 🔊 98

1. Why does the speaker think it's important to see animals in the wild?
   - ☐ a. to take photographs
   - ☐ b. to learn about how they live
   - ☐ c. to help the animals
   - ☐ d. to do a podcast

2. How does the speaker know there is a tiger?
   - ☐ a. They saw the shape of the paw in the mud.
   - ☐ b. They heard a tiger.
   - ☐ c. They saw a tiger.
   - ☐ d. The guide told them.

3. What is the speaker's opinion of rhinoceroses?
   - ☐ a. They are dangerous.
   - ☐ b. They are very fast.
   - ☐ c. They are very big.
   - ☐ d. They are amazing animals.

4. Why does the speaker think the roller bird is interesting?
   - ☐ a. It does flying tricks.
   - ☐ b. It's colorful.
   - ☐ c. It has pretty feathers.
   - ☐ d. He's never seen one before.

F **Discuss with a partner.**

1. Which endangered animal would you like to help?

2. Would you like to go on a safari? Why or why not?

3. Which animals would you like to see in the wild?

G **Listen and read. Complete the sentences.** 🔊 99

Many people love bird-watching. They like finding different types of birds (1) _____. When they see one, they take notes about the color of its (2) _____, the size of its (3) _____, and its (4) _____ to remember. Then they can look the birds up in a book to name them. Some birds are (5) _____, so bird-watchers also help to count them. If we don't take care of our world, some birds, like (6) _____, (7) _____, and (8) _____ may be endangered in the future.

WHAT CAN YOU DO? Color the stars.

I can listen for opinions. ⭐⭐⭐	**KEY** ⭐ I need help.
I can listen for attitudes. ⭐⭐⭐	⭐⭐ I can do this a little.
	⭐⭐⭐ I can do this well.

Get Ready to Speak

SPEAKING GOAL: Persuade

When we want someone to do or think something, we try to persuade them by sharing facts we know and our opinions.

A Read and listen to the conversation. Underline the persuasive words.  100

> **Speaking Tip**
> Use phrases like *I think*, *it's better*, and *we should* to persuade someone.

Helping Animals

Sam: Which animal do you want to help?

Ada: Oh! I think pandas are so cute! I want to help them. How about you?

Sam: I think we should help penguins because they're so funny.

Ada: I think it's better to help pandas. So many people helped them, now they aren't endangered anymore. I want to keep helping.

Sam: Oh! But I wanted to help penguins because the ice they live on is melting. They could be endangered soon.

Ada: Yes, but the forests where pandas live are very important for people and other animals.

Sam: You're right. It's very difficult to choose. All animals are important. We should help all animals in the wild!

B Discuss the questions with a partner.

1. Why does Ada think pandas need help?

2. Why does Sam think it's better to help the penguins?

3. What do they agree on in the end?

4. Do you think Ada or Sam is right? Why?

 NATURAL SPEECH: Interjections

Oh! is an interjection. Interjections show strong feelings. You can change the meaning of interjections by changing your intonation.

Oh! I think pandas are so cute! (excitement)

Oh! But I wanted to help penguins. (disappointment)  101

Listen to the interjections in **A**. Then write three sentences about an animal you want to help. Read your sentences to your partner and use intonation to change the meaning of your interjections.

Speak

C Think about a wild animal you want to help and why. Complete the chart. Add facts and opinions.

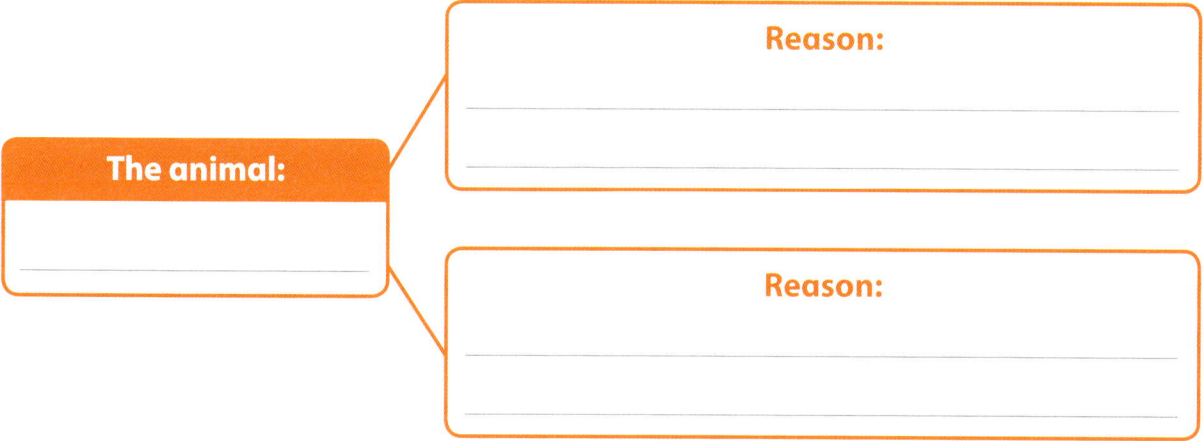

The animal:

Reason:

_____

_____

Reason:

_____

_____

D Write about your animal. Use your words from **C**. Choose new words, too.

1. Which animal do you want to help?

   _____

2. What's your opinion of the animal?

   _____

3. What are some facts about your animal?

   _____

4. What are the reasons you want to help your animal?

   _____

5. What words can you use to persuade someone to help?

   _____

 Ask your partner about his or her animal. Persuade your partner to help your animal.

WHAT CAN YOU DO? Color the stars.

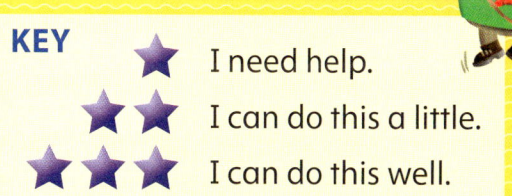

I can persuade someone. ★★★

I can use persuasive words. ★★★

KEY
★ I need help.
★★ I can do this a little.
★★★ I can do this well.

Our World

Hello

안녕

MY GOALS

UNIT 9

• Listen to the story
  The Traveler's Idea

• Listen for problems

UNIT 10

• Listen to the passage
  A Helpful Idea

• Listen for solutions

SPEAK

• Talk about problems

A Look at the picture.

1. What do you see?

2. What languages do you think they speak?

FUN FACT

Listen

Languages of the World

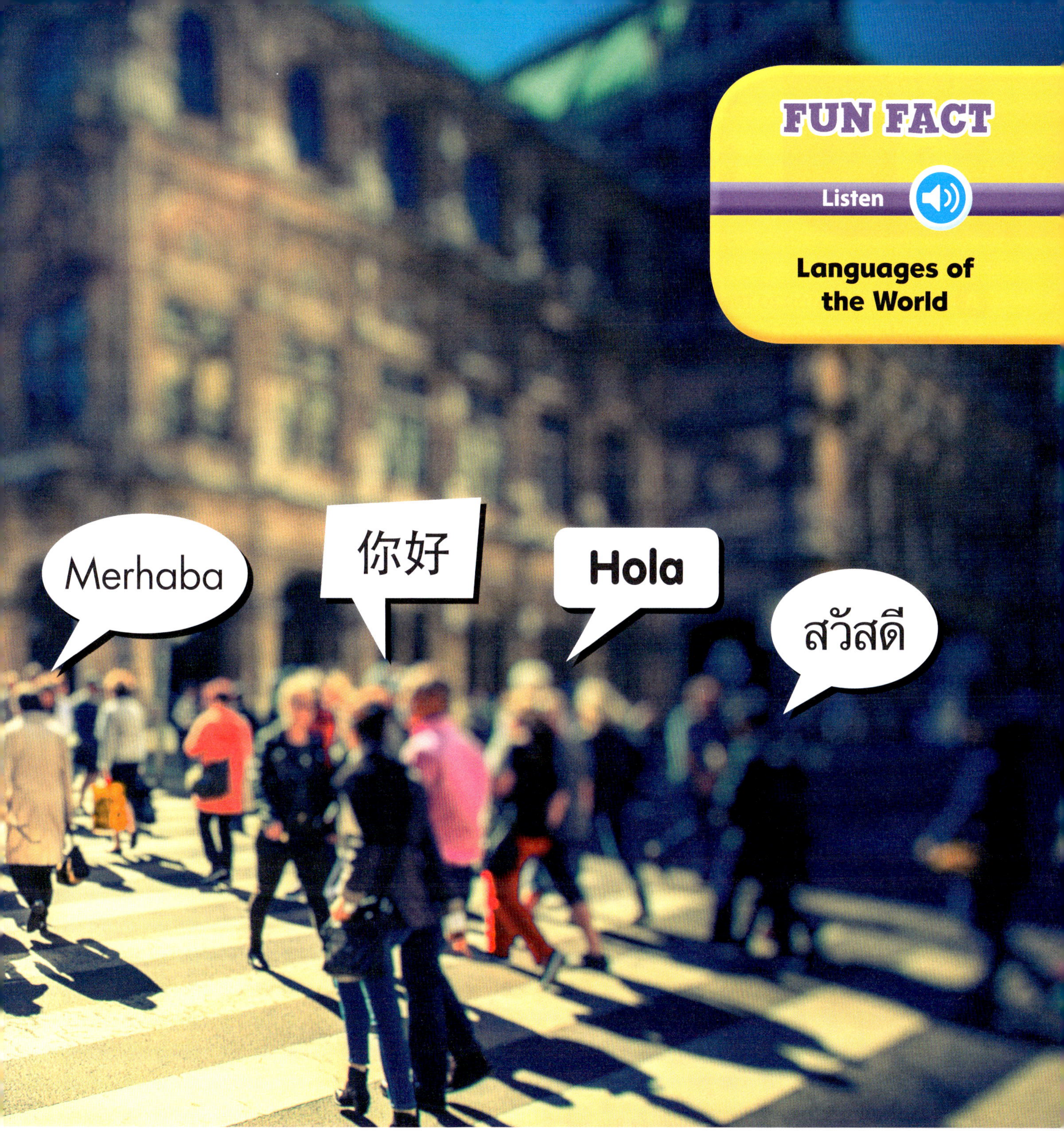

Merhaba
你好
Hola
สวัสดี

B Listen to the Fun Fact. Then answer the questions. 102

1. How many languages are there in the world?
2. How many languages does half the world speak?
3. How many languages do people speak in your country?

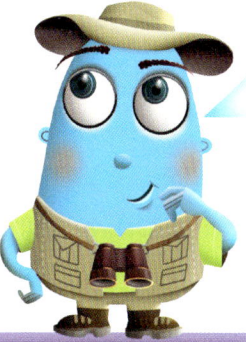

Think, Pair, Share
If you could speak one more language, which would you choose? Why?

Get Ready to Listen

Let's learn the **key words**.

A **Read and listen to the sentences. Look up the words you don't know in your dictionary.** 🔊 103

1. Our class is **diverse**, with students from many countries.
2. London has **immigrants** from all over the world.
3. **Kenya** is a country in East Africa.
4. Rob went to **Nepal** last year to hike mountains.
5. **New Zealand** is a country made of two main islands.
6. Last year we went on vacation to **Peru** in South America.
7. My best friend is from the city of Moscow in **Russia**.
8. England, Wales, Scotland, and Northern Ireland are all in **the UK**.

B **Listen and number.** 🔊 104

C **Listen and complete the sentences.** 🔊 105

I live in London. It's a very cool and (1) _____ city. There are a lot of (2) _____ here. In my class there is a boy from (3) _____ and a girl from (4) _____.

In our geography class we learn about each other's countries. It's fun to compare our lives and see how similar and different we are.

Listen

LISTENING GOAL: Listen for Problems

Many fiction stories and nonfiction passages have problems. A problem is something that goes wrong or makes things difficult for people. To find the problem when you listen, ask *What went wrong? What needs to be fixed?*

A Listen. What's the problem? Choose the correct answer. 🔊 106

1. ☐ a. The girl doesn't speak the language. ☐ b. The girl doesn't have a tablet.
2. ☐ a. The boy can't hear. ☐ b. The boy doesn't like the music.
3. ☐ a. Max didn't do his homework. ☐ b. Max can't find his bag.

B Listen to the story *The Traveler's Idea*. What happens? Take notes. 🔊 107

The Traveler's Idea

Notes

_____

_____

_____

_____

_____

_____

_____

_____

What questions can you ask to understand the **problem**?

Now put the sentences in order.

a. Mr. Green traveled to Nepal. ☐

b. Mr. Green visited Russia. ☐

c. The villagers sang songs and told stories together. ☐

WHAT CAN YOU DO? Color the stars.

I can listen to find out what a problem is. ⭐⭐⭐

I can understand the key words. ⭐⭐⭐

KEY
⭐ I need help.
⭐⭐ I can do this a little.
⭐⭐⭐ I can do this well.

Understand

Remember!
You can find the **problem** in a passage by asking *What went wrong?*

A Think about **The Traveler's Idea**. Answer the questions and discuss with the class.

1. How does Mr. Green learn about the problem in the village?

2. What is the problem in the village?

3. Why can't the children speak both languages?

B Listen to **The Traveler's Idea** again. Choose the correct answer. 🔊 108

1. What does Mr. Green do?
   - [ ] a. He travels to Kenya.
   - [ ] b. He studies languages.
   - [ ] c. He teaches English.
   - [ ] d. He writes travel books.

2. How many languages does Mr. Green speak with his family?
   - [ ] a. one
   - [ ] b. two
   - [ ] c. three
   - [ ] d. four

3. How many languages do people in Russia speak?
   - [ ] a. about 120
   - [ ] b. about 100
   - [ ] c. about 50
   - [ ] d. about 200

4. How do the villagers learn each other's languages?
   - [ ] a. They have lessons with a teacher.
   - [ ] b. They read books.
   - [ ] c. They tell stories and sing songs.
   - [ ] d. Mr. Green teaches them.

C Read the sentences. Then listen to **The Traveler's Idea** again. Choose the correct answer. 🔊 109

1. Mr. Green is from **the UK** / **Kenya** / **Russia**.

2. Mr. Green thinks Russia is **a diverse** / **an interesting** / **a beautiful** country.

3. The old people in the village were **sad** / **worried** / **surprised** that the children didn't speak the village language.

D Ask and answer the questions with a partner.

1. What words do you use that old people don't?

2. What are some things old people in your family want to teach you? Why?

3. Do songs and stories help you learn English?

Listen and complete the sentences. 🔊 110

the UK	Russia	diverse	Nepal	Kenya
	Peru	New Zealand	immigrants	

1. A lot of _____ come to the US.

2. There are many _____ languages in Africa.

3. _____ is very cold in the winter. The summers can be warm.

4. I'd love to go mountain climbing in _____

5. Sara showed me pictures of her vacation in _____

6. My brother went to school in _____. He loved it.

7. What language do they speak in _____

8. If you like outdoor activities, _____ is the best place for a vacation.

F **Listen to the advertisement for *Language Helper*. Complete the information.** 🔊 111

Do you need language help?

Are you:

- going to visit (1) _____

- going on a safari in (2) _____

- planning to go mountain climbing in (3) _____,
  (4) _____, or (5) _____

- an (6) _____ from
  (7) _____

Download the **Language Helper** app now!

Check our (8) _____ list of languages for every situation!

WHAT CAN YOU DO? Color the stars.

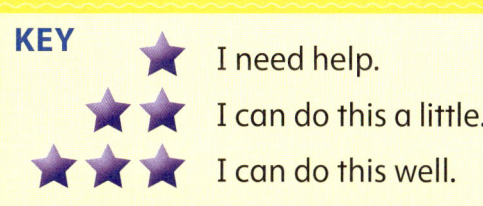

I can listen for a problem someone has. ⭐⭐⭐

KEY	
⭐	I need help.
⭐⭐	I can do this a little.
⭐⭐⭐	I can do this well.

Get Ready to Listen

Let's learn the **key words**.

A Read and listen to the sentences. Look up the words you don't know in your dictionary. 🔊 112

1. The **castle** walls were built very high to keep people safe.

2. Max became a **citizen** of the US, and now he can get a passport.

3. We ate so many delicious pizzas in **Italy** last year.

4. **Japan** is the country sushi comes from.

5. It's interesting to learn about the kings and queens who lived in **palaces**.

6. That **tower** is really tall. Do you know how many meters it is?

7. Our family **tradition** is to always have Sunday lunch together.

8. I love to eat kebabs when I'm in **Turkey**.

B Listen and write the number under the picture. 🔊 113

a. ____   b. ____   c. ____   d. ____

C Read each sentence. Then listen to the words. Two of the three key words are incorrect. Write the correct key word. 🔊 114

1. Pizza comes from this country.   _____

2. Kings and queens from some countries live in these.   _____

3. This country is famous for its kebabs.   _____

4. This is something that people in a particular place have done for a long time.   _____

Listen

LISTENING GOAL: Listen for Solutions

Most stories with problems have solutions. A solution is how a character fixes the problem. To find the solution when you listen, ask *How did the problem get fixed? What did the character do?*

A Listen. Number the pictures. 115

a.

b.

c.

B Listen to the passage *A Helpful Idea*. What is it about? Take notes. ◀) 116

Notes

_____

_____

_____

_____

_____

Now read. Choose T for True or F for False.

a. Bobby's dad is helping him prepare for his geography test. **T** **F**

b. Bobby can't remember the facts for the test. **T** **F**

c. Bobby's dad tells him to study more. **T** **F**

Who has a **solution** for Bobby's problem?

WHAT CAN YOU DO? Color the stars.

I can listen for solutions to a problem. ★★☆

I can understand all the key words. ★★★

KEY

★ I need help.

★★ I can do this a little.

★★★ I can do this well.

Understand

Remember!
The **solution** is how a person fixes a problem.

A Think about **A Helpful Idea**. Answer the questions and discuss with the class.

1. What problem does Bobby have?

2. How does Bobby's dad help fix the problem?

3. What did Bobby need to fix his problem?

4. What are some other ideas to fix Bobby's problem?

B Listen to **A Helpful Idea** again. Choose **T** for **True** or **F** for **False**. 🔊 117

1. Bobby is studying for a math test.	T	F
2. Bobby's dad wrote facts on pieces of paper when he was a student.	T	F
3. Bobby's dad tells Bobby to write the facts in a notebook.	T	F
4. Bobby puts the pieces of paper around the house.	T	F
5. Bobby writes *Italy* and *pizza* on one piece of paper.	T	F
6. Bobby's family always eats breakfast together.	T	F
7. Bobby's mom and dad ask him questions.	T	F
8. Bobby wasn't ready for his test.	T	F

C Read the sentences. Then listen to **A Helpful Idea** again. Complete the sentences. 🔊 118

1. Bobby needed to know each _____ and one fact for his test.

2. Bobby has a problem remembering the _____

3. It's a good idea to put the pieces of paper all _____

4. Bobby's family asked him questions _____

D Ask and answer the questions with a partner.

1. Do you think Bobby's way of studying would help you remember facts?

2. What ideas do you have for studying for tests?

3. Does your family help you study for tests? How?

Listen. Then read and choose the correct answer. 🔊 119

1. When the girl says *citizens*, she means

   ☐ a. people who have a passport for a country.

   ☐ b. children who go to school.

   ☐ c. parents of small children.

   ☐ d. people on vacation or tourists.

2. When the boy says *tower*, he means

   ☐ a. a wall.

   ☐ b. a house.

   ☐ c. a tall building.

   ☐ d. a big box.

3. When the man says *Japan*, he means

   ☐ a. a country in Europe.

   ☐ b. a country in Asia.

   ☐ c. a country in Africa.

   ☐ d. a country in South America.

4. When the woman says a *castle*, she means

   ☐ a. a person living in a city.

   ☐ b. an apartment in a village.

   ☐ c. a building that keeps people safe.

   ☐ d. a shop in a small town.

F **Look and listen. Choose the best description.** 🔊 120

1.

☐ a.　☐ b.　☐ c.　☐ d.

2.

☐ a.　☐ b.　☐ c.　☐ d.

3.

☐ a.　☐ b.　☐ c.　☐ d.

4.

☐ a.　☐ b.　☐ c.　☐ d.

WHAT CAN YOU DO? Color the stars.

I can listen for how the characters in a story fix a problem. ⭐⭐⭐

KEY

⭐ I need help.

⭐⭐ I can do this a little.

⭐⭐⭐ I can do this well.

Listening Check

Remember!
When you listen to a story, listen for **problems** and **solutions**. Listen and think about what went wrong and how the problem was fixed.

A Listen to the story **A Creative Solution**. What is it about? Take notes and choose the correct answer. 🔊 121

Notes

☐ a. facts about Russia

☐ b. a lost address book in Russia

B Listen to **A Creative Solution** again. Order the pictures. 🔊 122

a.

b.

c.

C Think about **A Creative Solution**. Then choose the correct answer.

1. You want to know what went wrong on the girls' vacation. What do you do?

   ☐ a. listen for problems   ☐ b. listen for solutions

2. You want to know how the girls fixed the problem. What do you do?

   ☐ a. listen for problems   ☐ b. listen for solutions

D Answer the questions and discuss your answers with the class.

1. What was Kate and Jenny's problem?

2. How did they fix the problem?

E Listen to **A Creative Solution** again. Choose the correct answer. 🔊 123

1. What did the girls do first when Kate lost her address book?
   - [ ] a. They called their parents.
   - [ ] b. They went to the police.
   - [ ] c. They went to the last place they visited.
   - [ ] d. They asked someone for help.

2. What did the girls think about the citizens of Russia?
   - [ ] a. They were interesting.
   - [ ] b. They were friendly.
   - [ ] c. They were fun.
   - [ ] d. They were helpful.

3. What was Kate's first idea?
   - [ ] a. act like she is opening and closing a book
   - [ ] b. use her cell phone to call home
   - [ ] c. use a Russian dictionary
   - [ ] d. go to the police and ask for help

4. What did Kate draw?
   - [ ] a. an address book
   - [ ] b. a dictionary
   - [ ] c. a book about Russia
   - [ ] d. an airplane

F Discuss with a partner.

1. Have you lost something important on vacation?
2. What problem did you fix last week?
3. How did you fix it?

G Listen and read. Complete the sentences. 🔊 124

I have a (1) _____ group of friends. They're from all over the world. My best friend is from (2) _____. Her parents came to the US as (3) _____ many years ago. One (4) _____ we have in our class is to do show-and-tell. Olga is from (5) _____. She talked about the Russian dolls she collects. Suki is from (6) _____. She showed us how to wear a kimono. David, from (7) _____, showed us pictures from Rome. I'm from (8) _____, and I talked about English food. I love hearing about what makes us all special.

WHAT CAN YOU DO? Color the stars.

I can listen for the problem in a story.
⭐⭐⭐

I can listen for how a problem is fixed.
⭐⭐⭐

KEY
⭐ I need help.
⭐⭐ I can do this a little.
⭐⭐⭐ I can do this well.

Get Ready to Speak

SPEAKING GOAL: Talk About Problems

When we have conversations, we can talk about problems. Talking about problems will help listeners understand you. They can also help you find solutions.

A Read and listen to the conversation. Underline the words that make the adjectives stronger. 🔊 125

> **Speaking Tip**
> Use words like *really*, *very*, and *so* before adjectives to make them stronger.

English Problems

Patrick: How are you today?

Meg: Not good. I'm <u>really</u> worried.

Patrick: Why? What's the matter?

Meg: I have English homework to do, and I don't know how to do it. English is very difficult for me.

Patrick: What's it about?

Meg: I have to learn my irregular verbs. It's so hard to do.

Patrick: Don't worry. I'll help you.

Meg: That's great. Thank you.

B Discuss the questions with a partner.

1. What is Meg's problem?
2. What does she think about the English homework?
3. What is Patrick good at?
4. What's the solution?
5. What homework do you always need help with?

NATURAL SPEECH: Emphasis

When you want to show emphasis, or strong feelings, you put more stress on some words. We stress words like *very*, *really*, and *so*.

English is **very** difficult. 🔊 126

Listen for the words with extra stress in **A** again. Then write three sentences about a problem. Practice using extra stress on some words with your partner.

Speak

C Think about a problem you had. Complete the chart with your ideas.

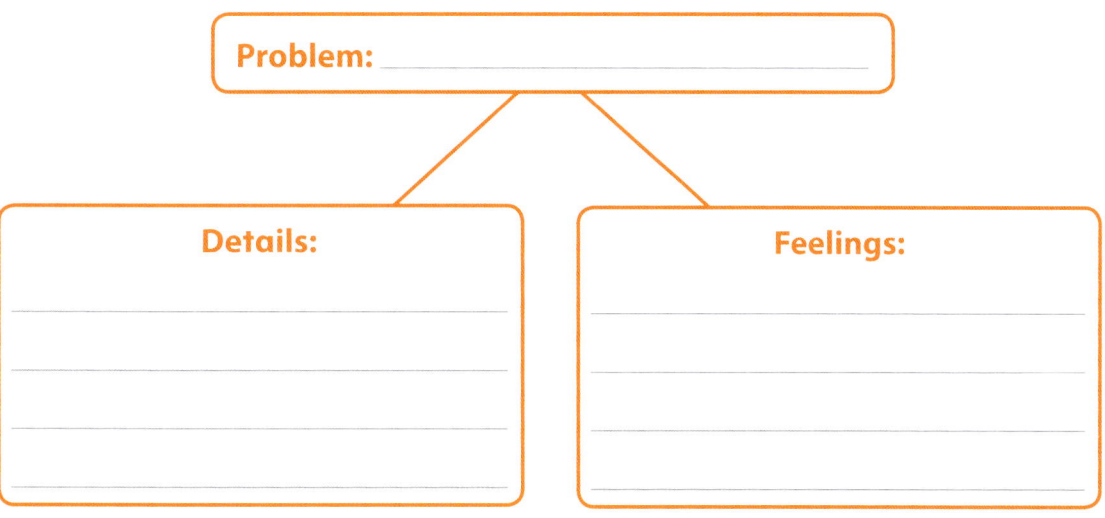

Problem: _____

Details:
_____
_____
_____

Feelings:
_____
_____
_____

D Write about your problem. Use your words from **C**. Choose new words, too.

1. What was your problem?

   _____

2. How did you feel?

   _____

3. Who did you talk to?

   _____

4. Why did you talk to them?

   _____

 Ask your partner about his or her problem. Help to find another solution. Then tell your partner your problem. Use words like *very*, *so*, and *really*.

WHAT CAN YOU DO?   Color the stars.

I can talk about a problem. ★★★

I can use and stress words to emphasize how I feel. ★★★

KEY
★ I need help.
★★ I can do this a little.
★★★ I can do this well.

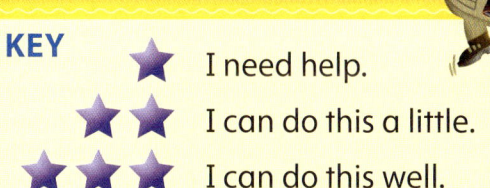

TOPIC
6

SCIENCE

Let's Do Better!

MY GOALS

UNIT 11

- Listen to the passage *Who's Been Here?*
- Listen for gist

UNIT 12

- Listen to the story *I Live Here, Too!*
- Listen for the theme

SPEAK

- Tell a personal story

 A Look at the picture.

1. What can you see?
2. What do you think happened to this place? Why?

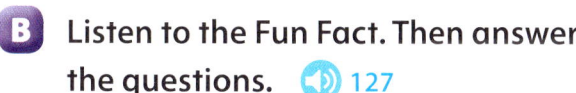

FUN FACT

Listen 🔊

Plastic Bags Everywhere!

B Listen to the Fun Fact. Then answer the questions. 🔊 127

1. How many plastic bags are used in the US?

2. Why are plastic bags bad for animals?

3. Do you think it's hard to not use plastic bags? Why or why not?

Think, Pair, Share
What can we do to use fewer plastic bags?

Get Ready to Listen

Let's learn the **key words**.

A Read and listen to the sentences. Look up the words you don't know in your dictionary. 🔊 128

1. My dog smells **awful** after swimming in the lake.
2. The toy is very soft and **furry**.
3. The **metal** lock is hard.
4. Many children have **plastic** toys.
5. Let's play with a **rubber** ball. It's softer than this one.
6. Clothes made from **silk** are soft and shiny.
7. I always have **sticky** hands after eating chocolate.
8. We use **wood** to make many things.

B Listen and number. 🔊 129

C Listen and complete the sentences. 🔊 130

Last week we had a class trip to our nearest beach to pick up trash. Sometimes the beach looks (1) _____ and messy. Each person had a bag to fill. Then we thought about how we could reuse some of the trash. I found some (2) _____ and a (3) _____ bag. The bag was really (4) _____, but after I washed it, it was like new!

Listen

LISTENING GOAL: Listen for Gist

The gist is what a listening is mostly about. To find the gist, look at the pictures, the title, and the activity questions. The first sentence of the listening can also help you know the gist. When you listen, ask *What is the speaker talking about?*

A Listen. What is the speaker talking about? Choose the correct answer. 🔊 131

1. ☐ a. reusing things ☐ b. shopping
2. ☐ a. camping in the forests ☐ b. taking care of the Earth
3. ☐ a. a party on the beach ☐ b. cleaning up after a party

Who's Been Here?

B Listen to the passage *Who's Been Here?*
What is it about? Take notes. 🔊 132

Notes
_____
_____
_____
_____
_____
_____

Now put the sentences in order.

a. The boy's team won the game.
b. The teacher asked the children to collect the trash.
c. The class painted a sign.

☐
☐
☐

What does the first sentence of the passage tell you?

WHAT CAN YOU DO? Color the stars.

I can listen for the gist to find out what the speaker is talking about. ⭐⭐⭐

I can understand all the key words. ⭐⭐⭐

KEY
⭐ I need help.
⭐⭐ I can do this a little.
⭐⭐⭐ I can do this well.

Understand

A Think about **Who's Been Here?** Answer the questions and discuss with the class.

1. How did the photo and the title help you understand the gist of the passage?

2. Look back at your notes. Which words helped you know what the passage was about?

3. How did the other activities on the page help you understand the gist of the passage?

B Listen to **Who's Been Here?** again. Choose the correct answer. 🔊 133

1. What was on the picnic table?
   - [ ] a. something sticky
   - [ ] b. something colorful
   - [ ] c. something furry
   - [ ] d. something plastic

2. What did the team find?
   - [ ] a. a silk kite
   - [ ] b. a silk shoe
   - [ ] c. a silk teddy bear
   - [ ] d. a silk doll's leg

3. Who was in the forest before?
   - [ ] a. chefs
   - [ ] b. children
   - [ ] c. hikers
   - [ ] d. teachers

4. What did the sign say?
   - [ ] a. Take Your Trash Away
   - [ ] b. Put Your Trash in the Trash Can
   - [ ] c. Throw Your Trash on the Ground
   - [ ] d. Please Keep the Forest Beautiful

C Read the sentences. Then listen to **Who's Been Here?** again. Choose the correct answer. 🔊 134

1. The forest looked **awful** / **beautiful** / **clean** when the students arrived.

2. The teddy bear's ear was **furry** / **rubber** / **sticky**.

3. The team found a **plastic** / **rubber** / **metal** shoe.

4. The furry thing was **square** / **rectangle** / **triangle** shaped.

D Ask and answer the questions with a partner.

1. Does your class go on class trips? Where do you go?

2. What was your favorite class trip?

3. Where do you think your class should go on the next class trip?

Listen and complete the sentences. 🔊 135

| metal | plastic | awful | furry | silk | sticky | rubber | wood |

1. Can you put this _____ food in the trash, please?

2. Max's _____ new coat is really nice.

3. We have our own _____ water bottles at school.

4. We can use the _____ blocks to build a tower.

5. Can I touch your _____ bag? It looks so soft.

6. Can you wash this _____ spoon and fork, please?

7. Is this toy made of _____

8. Sue put all her toys in a _____ box.

F **Listen to the art teacher's instructions. Fill in the missing information.** 🔊 136

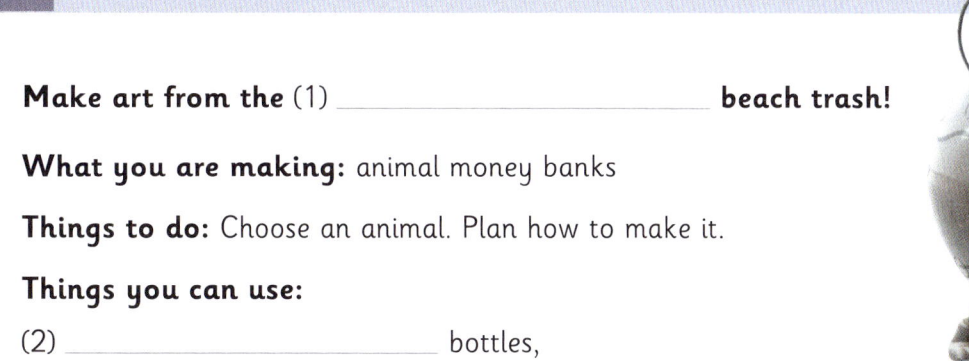

Make art from the (1) _____ **beach trash!**

What you are making: animal money banks

Things to do: Choose an animal. Plan how to make it.

Things you can use:

(2) _____ bottles,

(3) _____ and (4) _____ clothes,

(5) _____ and (6) _____ buttons,

(7) _____ bands

Remember: Clean up! Wash your (8) _____ hands.

WHAT CAN YOU DO? Color the stars.

I can use titles and pictures, and listen for important words to understand the gist. ⭐⭐⭐

KEY
⭐ I need help.
⭐⭐ I can do this a little.
⭐⭐⭐ I can do this well.

Get Ready to Listen

Let's learn the **key words**.

A Read and listen to the sentences. Look up the words you don't know in your dictionary. 🔊 137

1. I wear **cotton** dresses in the summer. They are really cool when it's hot.

2. Paula's bag is **full**. She can't fit any more books into it.

3. The **glass** bottle on the ground might break.

4. My dog is very **playful**. He loves chasing the ball when I throw it.

5. Scientists are worried because the air is **polluted** and unhealthy.

6. You don't need to **shout**! I can hear you.

7. Max heard a strange **sound** in the night. He couldn't sleep.

8. In the library you have to **whisper** because people are reading.

B Listen and write the number under the picture. 🔊 138

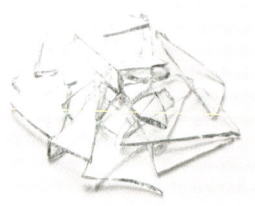

a. _____   b. _____   c. _____   d. _____

C Read each sentence. Then listen to the words. Two of the three key words are incorrect. Write the correct key word. 🔊 139

1. Monkeys are like this when they are having fun.   _____

2. If we throw trash in the ocean, the water becomes this.   _____

3. Sometimes if our class is noisy, my teacher does this.   _____

4. This is something you hear.   _____

Listen

LISTENING GOAL: Listen for the Theme

A theme is a lesson you can learn from a story. Usually the story doesn't tell you the theme. To find the theme after you listen, ask *What did the character learn? What did I learn?*

A Listen. What did the speaker learn? Choose the correct answer. 🔊 140

1. ☐ a. Working together can help you understand things.
   ☐ b. If you don't understand, try harder.
2. ☐ a. It's important to learn how to cross the road.
   ☐ b. If you are kind, somebody may be kind to you.

I Live Here, Too!

B Listen to the story *I Live Here, Too!* What is it about? Take notes. 🔊 141

Notes

Now read. Choose **T** for **True** or **F** for **False**.

1. Someone put their trash in the ocean.   T   F
2. Trash is dangerous to the animals in the ocean.   T   F
3. It's not good to swim in the ocean.   T   F

What details help you find the **theme**?

WHAT CAN YOU DO?   Color the stars.

I can listen for the theme of a story. ⭐⭐⭐
I can understand all the key words.   ⭐⭐⭐

KEY
⭐ I need help.
⭐⭐ I can do this a little.
⭐⭐⭐ I can do this well.

Understand

Remember!
The **theme** is a lesson everyone can learn from a story.

A Think about **I Live Here, Too!** Answer the questions and discuss with the class.

1. What lesson did Juan learn in the story?

2. What did you learn from the story?

3. How will you change because of this story?

4. What other lessons have you learned from stories?

B Listen to **I Live Here, Too!** again. Choose **T** for **True** or **F** for **False.** 🔊 142

1. Juan was swimming in the ocean.   T   F

2. There was a lot of trash in the ocean.   T   F

3. Juan touched a fish.   T   F

4. A T-shirt was around Juan's neck.   T   F

5. The turtle was happy after Juan helped it.   T   F

6. A boy threw a plastic bottle on the beach.   T   F

7. Juan shouted at the boy.   T   F

8. Juan learned his actions can make change.   T   F

C Read the sentences. Then listen to **I Live Here, Too!** again. Complete the sentences. 🔊 143

1. There was a lot of _____ in the ocean.

2. The turtle couldn't swim because the T-shirt was _____

3. Juan tells the turtle he's sorry that the turtle's home is _____

4. Juan tells the boy not to _____ on the beach.

D Ask and answer the questions with a partner.

1. How would you feel if you saw an animal in trouble?

2. What can you do to take care of the ocean?

3. Where do you see lots of trash?

4. What other stories do you know with a theme?

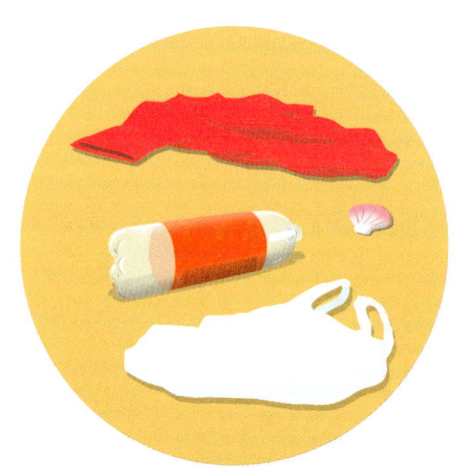

E **Listen. Then read and choose the correct answer.** 🔊 144

1. When the girl says her mom feels *awful*, she means

   ☐ a. her mom feels good.

   ☐ b. her mom feels bad and is sick.

   ☐ c. her mom is excited.

   ☐ d. her mom is angry.

2. When the boy says the air is *polluted*, he means

   ☐ a. the air is cool.

   ☐ b. the air is hot.

   ☐ c. the air is clean.

   ☐ d. the air is dirty.

3. When the man says the trash can is *full*, he means

   ☐ a. the trash can is empty.

   ☐ b. there is no more space in the trash can.

   ☐ c. the trash can is heavy.

   ☐ d. the trash can isn't clean.

4. When the woman says *playful*, she means

   ☐ a. having fun.

   ☐ b. be quiet.

   ☐ c. be helpful.

   ☐ d. play a game.

F **Look and listen. Choose the best description.** 🔊 145

1.

☐ a. ☐ b. ☐ c. ☐ d.

2.

☐ a. ☐ b. ☐ c. ☐ d.

3.

☐ a. ☐ b. ☐ c. ☐ d.

4.

☐ a. ☐ b. ☐ c. ☐ d.

WHAT CAN YOU DO? Color the stars.

I can listen to find out what a character learns in a story. ⭐⭐⭐

I can understand all the key words. ⭐⭐⭐

KEY

⭐ I need help.

⭐⭐ I can do this a little.

⭐⭐⭐ I can do this well.

Remember!
Listen for the **gist** to find out what someone is talking about. After listening to a passage identify the **theme** to learn a lesson.

A Listen to the passage **Earthships**. What is it about? Take notes. Then choose the correct answer. 🔊 146

Notes

_____

_____

_____

_____

☐ a. houses that are good for the Earth

☐ b. houses made from sand

B Listen to **Earthships** again. Order the pictures. 🔊 147

a. ☐   b. ☐   c. ☐

C Think about **Earthships**. Then choose the correct answer.

1. You want to know what the passage is generally about. What do you do?

   ☐ a. listen for the gist   ☐ b. listen for the theme

2. You want to know what the lesson of the passage is. What do you do?

   ☐ a. listen for the gist   ☐ b. listen for the theme

D Answer the questions and discuss your answers with the class.

1. What words and phrases helped you know what the passage was about? Did the picture give you any clues?

2. What is the important lesson of the passage?

E Listen to **Earthships** again. Choose the correct answer. 🔊 148

1. What is an Earthship?
   - ☐ a. a type of boat
   - ☐ b. a type of house
   - ☐ c. a type of garden
   - ☐ d. a type of transportation

2. What kind of shapes does Mike say the Earthships are?
   - ☐ a. interesting
   - ☐ b. square
   - ☐ c. pretty
   - ☐ d. boring

3. What are the outside walls made from?
   - ☐ a. rubber and plastic
   - ☐ b. glass and sand
   - ☐ c. rubber and sand
   - ☐ d. plastic and wood

4. Why do people collect the rain?
   - ☐ a. to save money
   - ☐ b. to build the house
   - ☐ c. to reuse the water
   - ☐ d. to give it to friends

F Discuss with a partner.

1. Would you like to live in an Earthship? Why or why not?

2. What would you build your Earthship from?

3. How do you think Earthships help the planet?

G Listen and read. Complete the sentences. 🔊 149

My dog, Zeke, is so (1) _____, and his ears feel like (2) _____. He's very (3) _____, so every day I take him to the park to throw a (4) _____ ball. One day he picked up a (5) _____ water bottle in the park. I (6) _____ for him to drop it, but Zeke kept trying to eat it. My dog was so excited, and he was making a funny (7) _____. I saw a woman running to me. Zeke was eating her water bottle! I felt (8) _____. I went to the store to get her a new water bottle.

WHAT CAN YOU DO? Color the stars.

I can listen for the gist to understand what the speaker is talking about. ⭐⭐⭐

I can listen for the theme to understand what the speaker learned. ⭐⭐⭐

KEY
⭐ I need help.
⭐⭐ I can do this a little.
⭐⭐⭐ I can do this well.

Get Ready to Speak

SPEAKING GOAL: Tell a Personal Story

When you tell a personal story, talk about something that happened to you and what you learned.

A Read and listen to Leah tell her personal story. Underline the past continuous.  150

> **Speaking Tip**
> Use the simple past (*I walked*) and past continuous (*I was walking*) to tell your personal story.

Doing Things Differently

By Leah Barnes

My friend Maria likes to help take care of the Earth. I stayed with her on Saturday night, and while I was watching TV she turned off the big light. I asked her why, and she told me that we didn't need it on. Later, while I was brushing my teeth, Maria turned off the water. She told me to only turn the water on when I needed it. Then, while I was lying in bed, I told her I was cold. She told me to put on a sweater! The next morning, as we were leaving the house, Maria gave me an umbrella. "I don't need this if we're going in the car," I said. Maria laughed. "It's only a 20-minute walk to the park! Come on."

B Discuss the questions with a partner.

1. What did Maria do while Leah was watching TV?

2. What was Leah doing when Maria turned off the water?

3. Why do you think Leah was cold?

4. What do you think Leah learned from Maria?

 NATURAL SPEECH: Simple Past Verbs

There are three ways to pronounce the -ed endings of regular simple past verbs: /t/, /d/, and /id/.

I **asked** her why.

Maria **turned** off the water. I turned it on when I **needed** it. 151

Listen for simple past endings in **A** again. Then write three sentences with simple past verbs. Say them with the correct pronunciation of the endings.

Speak

C Think about a personal story and what you learned from the experience. Complete the diagram with your ideas.

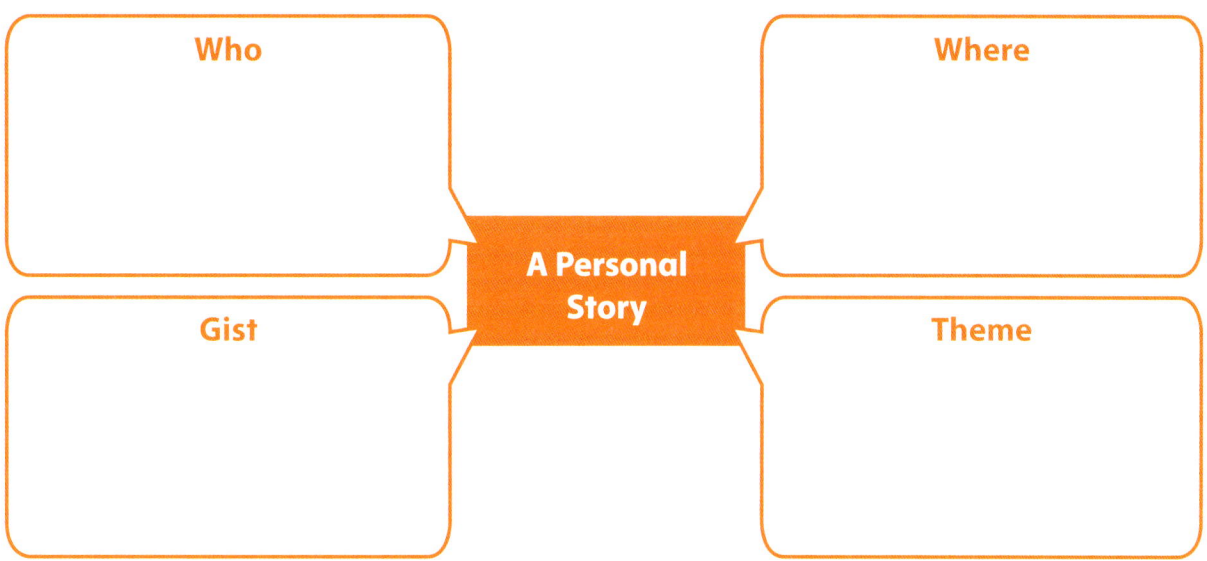

Who

Where

A Personal Story

Gist

Theme

D Write your story. Use your words from **C**. Use the past continuous, too.

1. What happened?

   _____

2. Where were you?

   _____

3. What lesson did you learn?

   _____

4. What were other people doing?

   _____

 Work in pairs. Tell your partner your story.

WHAT CAN YOU DO? Color the stars.

I can tell a personal story about a lesson I learned. ⭐⭐⭐

I can use the simple past and past continuous. ⭐⭐⭐

KEY
⭐ I need help.
⭐⭐ I can do this a little.
⭐⭐⭐ I can do this well.

Listening 5
WITH Speaking

Workbook

Jessica Finnis

OXFORD
UNIVERSITY PRESS

Listen

LISTENING GOAL:
Listen for Sequence

Remember!
The **sequence** is the order that things happen. Listen for words like *to begin with, suddenly, later,* and *in the end* to understand the sequence.

A Listen to the story **Pizza Pizza!** What is it about? Take notes. Then choose **T** for **True** or **F** for **False.** 🔊 152

Notes

_____

_____

_____

_____

_____

1. *Pizza Pizza!* is about children making pizza.   **T**   (**F**)

2. *Pizza Pizza!* is about parents surprising their children.   **T**   **F**

3. *Pizza Pizza!* is about children at a skate park.   **T**   **F**

B Think about **Pizza Pizza!** What is the sequence? Order the events.

a. Mr. and Mrs. Wright got a pizza.   [1]

b. Mr. and Mrs. Wright surprised their children.   [ ]

c. Mr. and Mrs. Wright did some chores.   [ ]

C Listen to **Pizza Pizza!** again. Choose the correct answer. 🔊 153

1. Where were Bob and Mary?
   - ☑ a. at the skate park
   - ☐ b. in their bedroom
   - ☐ c. at the movies

2. What time will Bob and Mary be home?
   - ☐ a. 8 p.m.
   - ☐ b. 2 p.m.
   - ☐ c. 6 p.m.

3. Where did Mr. and Mrs. Wright put the pizza box?
   - ☐ a. on the table
   - ☐ b. on the dishwasher
   - ☐ c. in the oven

4. Where was the pizza?
   - ☐ a. in the fridge
   - ☐ b. in the oven
   - ☐ c. on the table

D Think about **Pizza Pizza!** Answer the questions. Use full sentences.

1. What chores will Mary and Bob do when they get home?

   Mary and Bob will load the dishwasher and vacuum the floor.

2. What did Mr. and Mrs. Wright do while they waited for the pizza?

   _____

3. Why did Mr. and Mrs. Wright put the empty pizza box on the table?

   _____

4. How did Mary and Bob feel when they opened the pizza box?

   _____

5. What was the surprise?

   _____

E Listen. Choose the correct answer. 🔊 154

1. After lunch can you please (**hang out the clothes**) / **load the dishwasher**?
2. Look at all that mud! You need to **clean your shoes** / **do the laundry**.
3. Every evening we have to **take out the trash** / **clean the patio**.
4. Can you **vacuum the floor** / **feed the cat** before you go out, please?

F Listen and read. Complete the sentences. 🔊 155

Max has so much to do! He needs to (1) ___take out the trash___
before he does anything else. He also needs to
(2) _____. His mom asked him to
do that yesterday, but he forgot. He also forgot to
(3) _____, even though it is one
of his chores. If he can do these three things and also
(4) _____, then he can go to
his friend's party this afternoon. He needs to hurry!
Oh, no! He just saw a note his mom left for him
on the kitchen counter. Don't forget to
(5) _____
and (6) _____!
Will he ever finish?

Listen

LISTENING GOAL:
Listen and Make an Outline

Remember!
In your **outline**, use numbers and headings to show the main ideas and bullets to show details about the main ideas.

A Listen to the passage **Love and Thanks**. What is it about? Make an outline. Then choose the correct answer. 🔊 156

Outline

_____

_____

_____

_____

_____

1. What is the speaker talking about?
   ☐ a. Parents' Day in South Korea   ☐ b. Mother's Day in South Korea

2. Where is the speaker?
   ☐ a. in a classroom   ☐ b. at home

B Think about **Love and Thanks**. Then read the notes in your outline. Write **M** for **Main Idea** or **D** for **Details**.

1. do the chores   _D_   2. Parents' Day   _____   3. make paper flowers   _____

C Listen to **Love and Thanks** again. Choose the correct answer. 🔊 157

1. Parents' Day in South Korea is on May 5th.
   ☐ a. true   ✔ b. false   ☐ c. doesn't say

2. Min-Jun did the chores after school.
   ☐ a. true   ☐ b. false   ☐ c. doesn't say

3. Min-Jun will give his parents red paper flowers.
   ☐ a. true   ☐ b. false   ☐ c. doesn't say

4. Children wear special clothes for Parents' Day.
   ☐ a. true   ☐ b. false   ☐ c. doesn't say

5. Min-Jun will help cook a special meal.
   ☐ a. true   ☐ b. false   ☐ c. doesn't say

D Think about **Love and Thanks**. Complete the sentences with one, two, or three words.

1. Parents' Day is a day to say _____thank you_____ to parents.

2. Children are _____ to older people.

3. After school Min-Jun will _____

4. The paper flowers are _____

5. Min-Jun will put the paper flowers on his parents' _____

E Listen and read. Choose the correct answer. 🔊 158

> Tom wakes up thinking about the chores he has to do today. Then he remembers, today is Children's Day! At breakfast his parents wish him a happy day and ask, "What are you doing today, Tom?" "Nothing!" he answers happily as his mom (1) ____. "It's my free day!" Later he sees his dad in the garden. His dad is (2) ____ and (3) ____. Tom is a little bored and decides to help his dad. "Can I (4) ____ for you?" he asks. "It's Children's Day. No chores today," Dad says. "I know," Tom answers, "but helping you in the garden isn't a chore. It's fun!"

1. ☐ a. vacuums the floor
   ☑ b. clears the table

2. ☐ a. planting seeds
   ☐ b. cleaning the patio

3. ☐ a. planting seeds
   ☐ b. watering the plants

4. ☐ a. plant these seeds
   ☐ b. plant these flowers

F Listen and complete the sentences. 🔊 159

1. It's good to _____be helpful_____ all the time, not just on Parents' Day!

2. When you are in town, can you _____, please?

3. I'm feeling lazy today. I think I'll _____

4. Did you _____ before you watched TV?

Speak

Circle the sequence words in the instructions. Then think of your own instructions with sequence words. Tell your partner.

(First,) you must fold the card.

After that, draw and color a picture on the front.

Then write a special message to your parents inside.

Finally, give the card to your mom or dad.

Remember!
Use sequence words like *first*, *after that*, and *finally* to show steps in instructions.

WORKBOOK

UNIT 3

Listen

LISTENING GOAL:
Listen and Make Connections

Remember!
When you listen, ask *How is this similar to my life?* to **make connections**.

A Listen to the advertisement **Vacations Around the World**. What is it about? Take notes. Then choose **T** for **True** or **F** for **False**. 🔊 160

Notes

_____

_____

_____

_____

1. The advertisement is for family vacations. **T** **F**

2. The advertisement is only for beach holidays. **T** **F**

3. The advertisement is for activities, too. **T** **F**

B Think about **Vacations Around the World**. Which statements make a connection to the text? Choose the correct answers.

☐ a. I love doing activities with my family on vacation.

☐ b. I like learning something new on vacation.

☐ c. There are four people in my family.

C Listen to **Vacations Around the World** again. Choose the correct answer. 🔊 161

1. Where can you stay?

☐ a. on the beach or in the mountains

☐ b. the mountains

☐ c. the beach

2. What can you do in Argentina?

☐ a. go snorkeling

☐ b. go surfing

☐ c. go skiing

3. What can the children do at the kid's club in the mountains?

☐ a. go sledding

☐ b. go skiing

☐ c. go snowboarding

4. Where can you find more information?

☐ a. in a magazine

☐ b. on the website

☐ c. on TV

D Think about **Vacations Around the World**. Answer the questions. Use full sentences.

1. What can *Vacations Around the World* help you do?

   _____

2. What can families do on vacation?

   _____

3. What activities does the kid's club have in the mountains?

   _____

4. What can mom learn on a beach vacation?

   _____

5. What can the kids do while mom and dad relax?

   _____

E Listen. Choose the correct answer. 🔊 162

1. It's snowing. Let's go **snowboarding** / **sledding**.

2. **Windsurfing** / **Waterskiing** is really difficult. I can't stand up!

3. We love the ocean. We went **snorkeling** / **surfing** every day.

4. Toby **made a snowman** / **made a sandcastle**. Please don't fall on it!

F Listen and read. Complete the sentences. 🔊 163

Toby came back from a great vacation.
He went to the beach in Costa Rica.
The ocean was warm, so Toby went
(1) _____ every day.
He was lucky and saw lots of different
fish. On windy days, his dad went
(2) _____ with him.
It was very difficult. Toby was tired when he finished that activity.
After windsurfing, he (3) _____ with his little
sister on the beach. She was really sad when the ocean washed
it away! It's been snowing since Toby got home, so he went
(4) _____. He went to the park with
his sister to find the biggest hill. They had so much fun in
the sun and the snow.

Listen

LISTENING GOAL:
Listen and Draw
Conclusions

Remember!
A conclusion is a guess about what happened or what may happen. Use clues in the passage and your own experiences to **draw conclusions**.

A Listen to the story **Helpful Farmer Jones**. What is it about?
Take notes. Then choose the correct answer. 🔊 164

Notes

_____

_____

_____

1. What is the story about?

☐ a. Grandma Mabel makes apple pie.   ☐ b. how to make an apple pie

2. How many characters are there in the story?

☐ a. two   ☐ b. three

B Think about **Helpful Farmer Jones**. What conclusions can you draw about the story?
Choose the correct answers.

☐ a. It's winter in the story.

☐ b. Grandma Mabel was tired after she visited Farmer Jones.

☐ c. Grandma Mabel is going to make another apple pie.

C Listen to **Helpful Farmer Jones** again. Choose the correct answer. 🔊 165

1. There aren't any apples on Grandma Mabel's tree.

☐ a. true   ☐ b. false   ☐ c. doesn't say

2. Grandma Mabel's grandchildren are coming for a summer vacation.

☐ a. true   ☐ b. false   ☐ c. doesn't say

3. Farmer Jones helps make the apple pie.

☐ a. true   ☐ b. false   ☐ c. doesn't say

4. Grandma Mabel and Farmer Jones eat all the apple pie.

☐ a. true   ☐ b. false   ☐ c. doesn't say

5. Grandma Mabel has three grandchildren.

☐ a. true   ☐ b. false   ☐ c. doesn't say

D Think about **Helpful Farmer Jones**. Complete the sentences with one, two, or three words.

1. There are _____ hanging on Grandma Mabel's tree.

2. Farmer Jones has the apples in his _____

3. Grandma Mabel is _____ to make the pie.

4. Grandma Mabel _____ and went to sleep.

5. Grandma Mabel has to make another apple pie for her _____

E Listen and read. Choose the correct answer. 🔊 166

Last fall we went to a farm because it's the best (1) _____ to visit. In the morning we (2) _____. After we finished I helped the farmer by (3) _____ around the trees. In the afternoon we played a fun game with the apples. We put them in some water and tried to catch them with our mouths. In the evening it was really cold, so the farmer (4) _____. We sat next to it talking and learning all about the farm.

1. ☐ a. month   ☐ b. season

2. ☐ a. ate apples   ☐ b. picked apples

3. ☐ a. washing the apples   ☐ b. raking the leaves

4. ☐ a. made a fire   ☐ b. put on his coat

F Listen and complete the sentences. 🔊 167

1. The _____ look like they are dancing in the air.

2. Please take off your boots before the snow _____ on the floor.

3. Please don't _____ at your sister.

4. The _____ on the window look like glass.

Speak

Remember!
Use *Let's*, *How about*, *What about*, and *Why don't* to make suggestions.

Circle the suggestions in the conversation. Then think of your own conversation with suggestions. Tell your partner.

It's a sunny day. Why don't we go somewhere?

How about the farm?

Good idea. Let's ask Mom if it's OK.

Listen

LISTENING GOAL:
Listen and Visualize

A Listen to the passage **Five a Day**. What is it about? Take notes.
Then choose **T** for **True** or **F** for **False**. 🔊 168

Notes

_____

_____

_____

_____

_____

1. *Five a Day* is about making ice cream.   **T**   **F**

2. *Five a Day* is about making healthy fruit juices.   **T**   **F**

3. *Five a Day* is about staying healthy.   **T**   **F**

B Think about **Five a Day**. Which words help you visualize the juices?
Choose the correct answers.

☐ a. thicker   ☐ b. colorful   ☐ c. healthier

C Listen to **Five a Day** again. Choose the correct answer. 🔊 169

1. Who says it's important to follow the
   five-a-day rule?
   ☐ a. teachers
   ☐ b. doctors
   ☐ c. dentists

2. What is one of the speaker's favorite
   juices?
   ☐ a. mixed fruit juice
   ☐ b. vegetable juice
   ☐ c. watermelon juice

3. What is healthier than sugar?
   ☐ a. ice cream
   ☐ b. yogurt
   ☐ c. honey

4. How does the fruit look when it's
   mixing?
   ☐ a. pretty
   ☐ b. thick
   ☐ c. tasty

D Think about **Five a Day**. Answer the questions. Use full sentences.

1. What is a good way to get your five-a-day?

   _____

2. What fruits and vegetables does the speaker suggest to put in juice?

   _____

3. Why do you put yogurt in the juice?

   _____

4. Why do you put honey in the juice?

   _____

5. How does the speaker describe the glass of juice?

   _____

E Listen. Choose the correct answer. 🔊 170

1. Mi-Na eats **kimchi** / **garlic** with every meal.
2. Put in the **spices** / **red peppers** after the chicken is cooked.
3. **Papayas** / **Kiwis** grow on trees.
4. Max loves **watermelon** / **exotic fruits** in his fruit salad.

F Listen and read. Complete the sentences. 🔊 171

We know that eating a lot of fruits and vegetables is important for our health, but why is that? We studied a few foods to find out why. First there's (1) _____, which helps your hair grow and stay healthy. So put it in your food if you want long, thick hair. Some (2) _____, like (3) _____ and mango, are good for your heart. A strong heart helps you exercise. Lastly, (4) _____ is good for your eyes. It also helps your body if you are sick.

WORKBOOK
UNIT 6

Listen

LISTENING GOAL:
Listen to Classify and Categorize

Remember!
When you **classify** and **categorize**, you put things in groups to see how they are similar and different.

A Listen to the story **Everything and Anything**. What is it about? Take notes. Then choose the correct answer. 🔊 172

Notes

_____

_____

_____

1. What is the story about?

☐ a. shopping at the supermarket   ☐ b. a visit to a market

2. How does the Roberts family feel at the market?

☐ a. bored   ☐ b. excited

B Think about **Everything and Anything**. How can you categorize the things in the market?

a. pots, bowls, and mugs   _____

b. chili peppers, spinach, and melons   _____

c. T-shirts, jeans, and jackets   _____

C Listen to **Everything and Anything** again. Choose the correct answer. 🔊 173

1. The market was the same as a supermarket in the Roberts's country.

☐ a. true   ☐ b. false   ☐ c. doesn't say

2. All the clothes in the market were in the same place.

☐ a. true   ☐ b. false   ☐ c. doesn't say

3. Mrs. Roberts bought some flowers.

☐ a. true   ☐ b. false   ☐ c. doesn't say

4. The spices looked like small, colorful mountains.

☐ a. true   ☐ b. false   ☐ c. doesn't say

5. Charlie understood what the woman asked him.

☐ a. true   ☐ b. false   ☐ c. doesn't say

Unit 6 Workbook **101**

D Think about **Everything and Anything**. Complete the sentences with one, two, or three words.

1. The Roberts family went to a _____

2. The fruit and vegetables smelled like _____

3. The cans of tomatoes and cartons of juice were in the shape of a _____

4. The spices were in _____

5. Charlie had a _____ drink.

E Listen and read. Choose the correct answer. 🔊 174

Yesterday my mom told me to write a shopping list for the supermarket. She said, "We need a (1) _____, (2) _____, and a (3) _____." At the supermarket my mom said, "I'm sure we need one more thing, but I can't remember! Let's go home." On the way home she said, "Oh! (4) _____! That's what we forgot!" Then we both laughed.

1. ☐ a. carton of juice   ☐ b. a can of tomatoes
2. ☐ a. cinnamon   ☐ b. honey
3. ☐ a. melon   ☐ b. carton of orange juice
4. ☐ a. Cinnamon   ☐ b. Spices

F Listen and complete the sentences. 🔊 175

1. A _____ is a pretty orange color inside.

2. Please don't put any _____ in my dinner.

3. Strawberry _____ is my favorite.

4. Can you wash the _____ before you cook it, please?

Speak

Circle the transition phrases in the sentences. Then think of more sentences with transition phrases.

Anna: Here is Sue to talk about exotic fruit in Thailand.

Sue: Thank you, Anna. Mangoes are a very popular fruit from Thailand. They are great for making juices.

> **Remember!**
> Use transition phrases when you give a group presentation.

WORKBOOK

UNIT 7

Listen

LISTENING GOAL:
Listen for Opinions

Remember!
A person's **opinion** tells us what they think or feel about something.

A Listen to the passage **The Science of Birds**. What is it about? Take notes. Then choose the correct answer. 🔊 176

Notes

_____

_____

_____

_____

1. What is the passage about?

☐ a. eagles ☐ b. fish

2. What's the homework?

☐ a. write about the eagles ☐ b. make a presentation

B Think about **The Science of Birds**. Which sentence is an opinion?

☐ a. Eagles are some of the largest birds.

☐ b. Eagles are really interesting.

☐ c. Some eagles have wings over two meters long.

C Listen to **The Science of Birds** again. Choose the correct answer. 🔊 177

1. Eagles like to live near water.

☐ a. true ☐ b. false ☐ c. doesn't say

2. Eagles can't see very well.

☐ a. true ☐ b. false ☐ c. doesn't say

3. Eagles lay two or three eggs.

☐ a. true ☐ b. false ☐ c. doesn't say

4. Eagles have strong beaks.

☐ a. true ☐ b. false ☐ c. doesn't say

5. Some eagles eat small animals and birds.

☐ a. true ☐ b. false ☐ c. doesn't say

D Think about **The Science of Birds**. Complete the sentences with one, two, or three words.

1. The teacher thinks eagles are _____ birds.

2. Eagles have _____ feathers on their body.

3. The eagle's _____ are two meters long.

4. An eagle can see a _____ from very high up.

5. Please choose _____ for the next science lesson.

6. The teacher would do a presentation on _____

E Listen and read. Choose the correct answer. 🔊 178

Last week when I was at the Bird Zoo, I bought a (1) _____.
It's not real, of course! It's made of plastic but it's very pretty.
The (2) _____ are bright pink, the (3) _____ is black, and it's
standing on its right leg. I think I'll start collecting toy birds
because the flamingo looks really nice by my bed. I saw a
white (4) _____ at the store that is so pretty. Maybe I can
buy that next time.

1. ☐ a. swan   ☐ b. flamingo
2. ☐ a. wings   ☐ b. feathers
3. ☐ a. beak   ☐ b. body
4. ☐ a. swan   ☐ b. peacock

F Listen and complete the sentences. 🔊 179

1. _____ can see very well.

2. The police found the penguin after it _____ from the zoo.

3. Some _____ are smaller than a finger.

4. I really enjoyed the presentation on _____ in science class yesterday.

5. I want to have _____ in the winter. They will keep me warm.

6. Do birds use their _____ to smell?

Listen

LISTENING GOAL:
Listen for Attitudes

Remember!
A person's **attitude** can tell you *how* they feel about something.

A Listen to the story **King of the Rainforest**. What is it about? Take notes.
Then choose **T** for **True** or **F** for **False**. 🔊 180

Notes

_____

_____

_____

_____

1. The story is about animals in the wild.   **T   F**

2. The story is about a gorilla and a monkey playing together.   **T   F**

3. The story is about animals helping each other.   **T   F**

B Think about **King of the Rainforest**. What is the gorilla's attitude to the monkey?
Choose the correct answers.

☐ a. At the beginning, the gorilla is angry with the monkey.

☐ b. The gorilla is excited to see the monkey.

☐ c. At the end of the story, the gorilla is friendly to the monkey.

C Listen to **King of the Rainforest** again. Choose the correct answer. 🔊 181

1. Why are the small animals scared of the gorilla?

   ☐ a. because he's big and shouts

   ☐ b. because he's always angry

   ☐ c. because he's strong

2. How does the gorilla feel when he wakes up?

   ☐ a. worried

   ☐ b. angry

   ☐ c. surprised

3. What does the monkey say he'll do for the gorilla?

   ☐ a. do a trick

   ☐ b. help him one day

   ☐ c. play with him

4. How does the monkey break the net?

   ☐ a. with his hands

   ☐ b. with a stone

   ☐ c. with his teeth

D Think about **King of the Rainforest**. Answer the questions. Use full sentences.

1. Why did the gorilla shout, "I'm the king of the rainforest"?

_____

2. What did the monkey do to the gorilla?

_____

3. What was the monkey doing when he saw the gorilla in the net?

_____

4. Why couldn't the gorilla escape?

_____

5. Why does the monkey help the gorilla?

_____

E Listen. Choose the correct answer. 🔊 182

1. Can we go and see the **pandas** / **penguins** first, please?
2. I think hands are more useful than **wings** / **paws**.
3. Paul has pictures of **penguins** / **rhinoceroses** in his bedroom.
4. Animals that are **in the wild** / **endangered** need our help.

F Listen and read. Complete the sentences. 🔊 183

I learned two facts from a zookeeper today. (1) _____
don't have (2) _____. They have hands with fingers
like we do. (3) _____, some gorillas use sticks to dig
for their food. I also learned that (4) _____ can weigh
more than thirty men! They only eat plants and fruit, too. We share this
planet with animals. I think it's important to understand how they live.

Speak

Remember!
Use words like *it's better* and
we should to persuade someone.

**Circle the persuasive phrases in the conversation. Then think
of reasons zoos are good or bad. Tell your partner.**

I think it's better to see animals in the wild because we can understand
how they live.

We should make sure that animals have everything they need at the zoo.

Listen

LISTENING GOAL:
Listen for Problems

Remember!
Think about what's
wrong in the story
to find the **problem**.

A Listen to the story **A Walk in the Forest**. What is it about? Take notes.
Then choose **T** for **True** or **F** for **False**. 🔊 184

Notes

_____

_____

_____

_____

_____

1. The story is about traveling to the UK.   **T**   **F**

2. The story is about how to use a map.   **T**   **F**

3. The story is about getting lost.   **T**   **F**

B Think about **A Walk in the Forest**. What is the problem? Choose the correct answer.

☐ a. The children couldn't find their way back to their parents.

☐ b. The weather was very bad.

☐ c. They didn't have any food or water.

C Listen to **A Walk in the Forest** again. Choose the correct answer. 🔊 185

1. What time did the parents tell the children to be back?

   ☐ a. by six o'clock

   ☐ b. before dark

   ☐ c. by four o'clock

2. How did they feel when they knew they were lost?

   ☐ a. excited

   ☐ b. scared

   ☐ c. surprised

3. What lights did they see?

   ☐ a. lights on a car

   ☐ b. a flashlight

   ☐ c. a streetlight

4. How did they get back to their parents?

   ☐ a. Their parents found them.

   ☐ b. They stopped a car to ask.

   ☐ c. They rode in a car.

D Think about **A Walk in the Forest**. Answer the questions. Use full sentences.

1. What time did the children start walking back?

   _____

2. Why were they scared?

   _____

3. How did they know they were lost?

   _____

4. How did they know they were close to a road?

   _____

5. How did they feel when they returned to the tent?

   _____

E Listen. Choose the correct answer. 🔊 186

1. Connor went hiking in the mountains of **New Zealand** / **Peru**.
2. What does the word *diverse* / *immigrant* mean?
3. The winters in **Russia** / **the UK** are really long.
4. We are learning about **Kenya** / **Nepal** in geography class.

F Listen and read. Complete the sentences. 🔊 187

In geography class we learned about the colors and shapes of flags and their meanings. Many flags have red, blue, and green in them. Red means love, blue means water and the sky, and green means nature. Many flags have stars, squares, and crosses on them, too. The flag of (1) _____ has red and white squares. The flag of (2) _____ has four red stars on it. The flag of (3) _____ has a red cross on it. The flag of (4) _____ is the only flag that is not a square or rectangle.

Listen

LISTENING GOAL:
Listen for Solutions

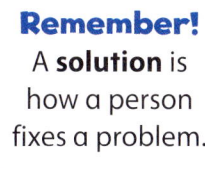

Remember!
A **solution** is
how a person
fixes a problem.

A Listen to the passage **Learning from Mistakes**. What is it about?
Take notes. Then choose the correct answer. 🔊 188

Notes

_____

_____

_____

1. What is the story about?

☐ a. A boy is trying to buy some things.   ☐ b. A boy is visiting a castle.

2. What does the boy use to help him in the store?

☐ a. a dictionary   ☐ b. his cell phone

B Think about **Learning from Mistakes**. How does Ali solve his problem?
Choose the correct answers.

☐ a. He checks the words on his phone and tries to say them.

☐ b. The woman helps him.

☐ c. He doesn't get what he needs. He's too shy to ask.

C Listen to **Learning from Mistakes** again. Choose the correct answer. 🔊 189

1. Ali wants to practice his English.

☐ a. true   ☐ b. false   ☐ c. doesn't say

2. Ali isn't worried because he has his phone.

☐ a. true   ☐ b. false   ☐ c. doesn't say

3. Ali buys a newspaper.

☐ a. true   ☐ b. false   ☐ c. doesn't say

4. The woman is friendly and helpful.

☐ a. true   ☐ b. false   ☐ c. doesn't say

5. Ali learns English at school in Turkey.

☐ a. true   ☐ b. false   ☐ c. doesn't say

D Think about **Learning from Mistakes**. Complete the sentences with one, two, or three words.

1. Ali wants to buy some paper, an envelope, and _____

2. Ali _____ the English words on his phone.

3. Ali is _____ when the woman gives him a newspaper.

4. The word _____ is difficult for Ali to say.

5. He chooses a _____ of Windsor Castle.

6. Ali thinks making _____ helps you learn.

E Listen and read. Choose the correct answer. 🔊 190

> I watched a TV show called *Eating* (1) _____. It was about what people eat in different countries. In (2) _____ many people love pasta and ice cream. In (3) _____ they share salads and small dishes. In (4) _____ they eat soups and have small dishes, too. I love eating, and I'd be happy with all these traditions in my home!

1. ☐ a. *Traditions*   2. ☐ a. Italy   3. ☐ a. Japan   4. ☐ a. Japan
   ☐ b. *at Home*   ☐ b. Japan   ☐ b. Turkey   ☐ b. the UK

F Listen and complete the sentences. 🔊 191

1. I bought my brother a really interesting book about _____

2. If you go to that town, you have to visit the _____ on the hill.

3. Ryan climbed the _____ to see the view.

4. Sometimes to become a _____ of another country you need to take a test.

5. What is your favorite _____ from Turkey?

6. My best friend went skiing in _____ for her vacation.

Speak

Remember!
When you talk about problems, use *really*, *very*, and *so* before adjectives to make them stronger.

Circle the words that make the adjectives stronger.
Then think of a problem. Tell your partner.

I'm very worried about starting my new Spanish lessons.
I'm so shy, but I like the language.

Listen

LISTENING GOAL:
Listen for Gist

Remember!
The **gist** is what a listening is mostly about. Pictures, the title, activity questions, and the first sentence can help you know the gist.

A Listen to the news report **Great Ideas**. What is it about? Take notes. Then choose **T** for **True** or **F** for **False.** 🔊 192

Notes

_____

_____

_____

_____

1. The Love Your Forest group wants to grow trees.   **T   F**
2. The Love Your Forest group picks up trash.   **T   F**
3. The Love Your Forest group has many ideas.   **T   F**

B Think about **Great Ideas**. What is the gist of the news report? Choose the correct answer.

☐ a. Activities for children to do on vacation.

☐ b. Ideas to help keep beautiful places clean.

☐ c. Activities for tourists in the park.

C Listen to **Great Ideas** again. Choose the correct answer. 🔊 193

1. What does the Love Your Forest group want to keep clean?

☐ a. parks, forests, and beaches

☐ b. stores and schools

☐ c. cities and neighborhoods

2. What does the group give to people who pick up trash?

☐ a. toys

☐ b. food and drinks

☐ c. books and maps

3. What will the children make at the Trash Store?

☐ a. pictures

☐ b. flowers

☐ c. faces

4. What does Love Your Forest want groups around the world to do?

☐ a. visit the store

☐ b. share their ideas

☐ c. help them

D Think about **Great Ideas**. Answer the questions. Use full sentences.

1. What was the group's first idea?

_____

2. What was the group's second idea?

_____

3. Where will the group put the flowers?

_____

4. What will children do in the Trash Store?

_____

5. What will the faces look like?

_____

E Listen. Choose the correct answer. 🔊 194

1. At school we have **metal** / **plastic** spoons and forks.
2. This chocolate cake is **awful** / **sticky**. I don't want any more.
3. I made a toy train from **metal** / **wood** blocks.
4. Is that **rubber** / **furry** ball for the cat to play with?

F Listen and read. Complete the sentences. 🔊 195

I was interested in Ben's talk about reusing things
and not throwing them away. I wanted to try
it, so I cut a large (1) _____
water bottle in half. Then I found an old
(2) _____ red hat and cut it
up. I stuck the furry material around the bottle.
Then I got a (3) _____ lid from
a jar, painted it, and put it on top to cover the
bottle. I put all my pens and pencils in it. I think it
looks really cool! But when my brother saw it, he
said, "That looks (4) _____!"
I guess Ben's ideas aren't for everyone!

Listen

LISTENING GOAL:
Listen for the Theme

Remember!
To identify the **theme**, ask *What did the character learn?*

A Listen to the story **I Told You!** What is it about? Take notes.
Then choose the correct answer. 🔊 196

Notes

_____

_____

_____

_____

1. What is the story about?

☐ a. taking care of water   ☐ b. a rainy day

2. Where is the story set?

☐ a. in a village   ☐ b. in a city

B Think about **I Told You!** What do the people learn? Choose the correct answer.

☐ a. They learn that water is very important.

☐ b. They learn there is always more water.

☐ c. They learn that they don't need water.

C Listen to **I Told You!** again. Choose the correct answer. 🔊 197

1. Sandip knew water was very important for the village.

☐ a. true   ☐ b. false   ☐ c. doesn't say

2. The people in the village listened to Sandip.

☐ a. true   ☐ b. false   ☐ c. doesn't say

3. Sandip learned about water at school.

☐ a. true   ☐ b. false   ☐ c. doesn't say

4. The children didn't play with the water.

☐ a. true   ☐ b. false   ☐ c. doesn't say

5. The villagers were happy when it rained.

☐ a. true   ☐ b. false   ☐ c. doesn't say

D Think about **I Told You!** Complete the sentences with one, two, or three words.

1. Water is very important for _____
2. The villagers used _____ water.
3. _____ the children threw the water.
4. The villagers wanted to wash their _____ clothes.
5. The villagers were happy to hear _____ of rain.
6. The villagers put the water in _____

E Listen and read. Choose the correct answer. 🔊 198

It's not only trash that makes our Earth (1) _____. Noise can be a problem too. The (2) _____ of transportation, building new houses, and phones ringing is everywhere in our cities. People are also loud. They play loud music in the street and (3) _____ on their phones in restaurants. In our busy world, it is very difficult to find a quiet place. Next time you are out of the city, take some time to stop and listen to the sounds of the birds and the wind in the trees. (4) _____ to your friends and enjoy the quiet.

1. ☐ a. polluted   2. ☐ a. noise   3. ☐ a. shout   4. ☐ a. talk
   ☐ b. awful   ☐ b. sound   ☐ b. whisper   ☐ b. whisper

F Listen and complete the sentences. 🔊 199

1. The cat is always _____ after it has its food.
2. I don't like the _____ at a soccer game.
3. The lake looks really _____
4. It's not good to _____ when you are working in a group.
5. The movie theater is _____. Let's go to the swimming pool.
6. I sleep really well under my new _____ blanket.

Speak

Remember!
Use the simple past and past continuous to tell your personal story.

Circle words in the simple past and past continuous in the sentences below. Then think of your own story. Use the simple past and past continuous. Tell your partner.

While I was playing on the playground, I picked up some trash.

My friends laughed when I put their trash in the can.

Dictionary

Definitions based on the *Oxford Basic American Dictionary for Learners of English.*

A

awful *adjective* very bad

B

beak *noun* the hard pointed part of a bird's mouth

C

can *noun* a metal container for food or a drink that keeps it fresh: *a can of tomatoes*

carton *noun* a container made of very thick paper (called cardboard) or plastic: *a carton of juice*

castle *noun* a large old building that was built in the past to keep people safe from attack

chili pepper *noun* a small green or red vegetable that has a very strong hot taste

cinnamon *noun* a brown powder that is used to give flavor to sweet foods

citizen *noun* a person who belongs to a country or a city

clean *verb* to remove the dirt or marks from something; to make something clean: *clean my shoes/clean the patio*

clear *verb* to remove things from a place because you do not want or need them there: *clear the table*

cotton *noun* a natural cloth that is made from the soft white hairs around the seeds of a plant that grows in hot countries

D

diverse *adjective* very different from each other

do *verb* to carry out an action: *do the laundry*

dry *verb* to become or make something dry: *dry the dishes*

E

eagle *noun* a very large bird that can see very well. It catches and eats small birds and animals

endangered *adjective* (used about animals, plants, etc.) in danger of disappearing from the world (becoming extinct)

escape *verb* to get free from someone or something

exotic *adjective* strange or interesting because it comes from another country: *exotic fruit*

F

feather *noun* one of the light, soft things that grow in a bird's skin and cover its body

feed *verb* to give food to a person or an animal: *feed the cat*

flamingo *noun* a large pink and red bird that has long legs and stands in water

full *adjective* with a lot of people or things in it, so that there is no more space

furry *adjective* covered with fur

G

garlic *noun* a plant like a small onion with a strong taste and smell, which you use in cooking

glass *noun* hard material that you can see through. Bottles and windows are made of glass

gorilla *noun* an African animal like a very big black monkey

H

hang out *phrasal verb* to put wet clothes, etc. outdoors so that they can dry: *hang out the clothes*

helpful *adjective* wanting to help; useful

honey *noun* the sweet food that is made by some insects (called bees)

hummingbird *noun* a small, brightly colored bird that lives in warm countries and that can stay in one place in the air by beating its wings very fast

I

icicle *noun* a long piece of ice that hangs down from something

immigrant *noun* a person who comes to another country to live there

Italy *noun* a country in southern Europe

J

Japan *noun* an island country in eastern Asia

K

Kenya *noun* a country in eastern Africa

kimchi *noun* a type of spicy Korean food made with cabbage, onions, peppers, etc.

kiwi *noun* a small, green fruit with black seeds and rough, brown skin

L

load *verb* to put things in or on something, for example a car or a ship: *load the dishwasher*

M

mail *verb* to send a letter or package to someone: *mail a package*

make *verb* to produce or create something: *make a sandcastle/make a snowman/made a fire*

melon *noun* a big, round, yellow or green fruit with a lot of seeds inside

melt *verb* to warm something so that it becomes liquid; to get warmer so that it becomes liquid

metal *noun* a solid substance that is usually hard and shiny, such as iron, silver, or gold

N

Nepal *noun* a country in southern Asia

New Zealand *noun* an island country in the southern Pacific Ocean

P

palace *noun* a very large house where a king or queen lives

panda *noun* a large black and white animal that lives in China

papaya *noun* a tropical fruit with yellow and green skin and round black seeds

paw *noun* the foot of an animal, for example a dog or a cat

peacock *noun* a large bird with beautiful long blue and green feathers in its tail

penguin *noun* a black and white bird that lives in very cold places. Penguins can swim but they cannot fly

Peru *noun* a country in western South America

pick *verb* to take a flower, fruit, or vegetable from the place where it grows: *pick apples*

plant *verb* to put plants or seeds in the ground: *plant seeds/plant flowers*

plastic *noun* an artificial material that is used for making many different things

playful *adjective* full of fun; not serious

polluted *adjective* (used to describe air, rivers, etc.) dirty and dangerous

R

rake *verb* to use a tool with a long handle (called a rake) to collect leaves or to make the soil flat: *raking the leaves*

red pepper *noun* a red vegetable that is almost empty inside

rhinoceros *noun* a big, wild animal from Africa or Asia, with thick skin and a horn on its nose

rubber *noun* a strong material that we use to make things like car tires

Russia *noun* a country in both northern Asia and eastern Europe

S

season *noun* one of the four parts of the year (called spring, summer, fall, and winter)

shout *verb* to speak very loudly

silk *noun* a soft, smooth cloth made from a substance that an insect (called a silkworm) makes

sled *verb* to sit in a small vehicle with pieces of metal or wood instead of wheels (called a sled), in order to move over snow: *sledding down snowy hills*

snorkel *verb* to use a short tube to breathe through while swimming just below the surface of water: *go snorkeling*

snowball *noun* a ball of snow that children throw at each other: *throw snowballs*

snowboard *verb* to move down mountains that are covered in snow using a large board (called a snowboard) that you fasten to both your feet: *go snowboarding*

snowflake *noun* one piece of falling snow

sound *noun* something that you hear

spice *noun* a powder of the seeds from a plant, which you can put in food to give it a stronger taste

spinach *noun* a vegetable with big, green leaves

stay *verb* to be in the same place and not go away: stays at home

sticky *adjective* covered with a substance that can stick to things

surf *verb* to ride on waves while standing on a surfboard: *go surfing*

swan *noun* a big, white bird with a very long neck. Swans live on rivers and lakes

T

take *verb* to move something or go with someone to another place: *take out the trash*

the UK *noun* the United Kingdom; a country in western Europe that includes England, Wales, Scotland, and Northern Ireland

tower *noun* a tall, narrow building or a tall part of a building

tradition *noun* something that people in a particular place have done or believed for a long time

Turkey *noun* a country in both southern Europe and western Asia

V

vacuum *verb* to clean a floor using a vacuum cleaner: *vacuums the floor*

W

water *verb* to give water to plants: *water the plants*

watermelon *noun* a big, round fruit with a thick, green skin. It is pink inside with a lot of black seeds

waterski *verb* to move fast over water on long boards (called waterskis), pulled by a boat: *go waterskiing*

whisper *verb* to speak very quietly to someone, so that other people cannot hear what you are saying

wild *noun* a natural area that is not controlled by people: *in the wild*

windsurf *verb* to move over water on a special board with a sail: *go windsurfing*

wing *noun* one of the two parts that a bird or an insect uses to fly

wood *noun* the hard substance that trees are made of

Y

yogurt *noun* a thick, liquid food made from milk

Syllabus

Topic	Unit	Listening Goal	Key Words	Speaking Goal
TOPIC 1 Helping Out	Unit 1	Listen for sequence	*clean my shoes, clean the patio, do the laundry, feed the cat, hang out the clothes, load the dishwasher, take out the trash, vacuum the floor*	Give instructions
	Unit 2	Listen and make an outline	*clear the table, dry the dishes, helpful, mail a package, plant flowers, plant seeds, stay at home, water the plants*	Focus: Sequence
TOPIC 2 Let's Go on Vacation!	Unit 3	Listen and make connections	*make a sandcastle, make a snowman, sledding, snorkeling, snowboarding, surfing, waterskiing windsurfing*	Make suggestions
	Unit 4	Listen and draw conclusions	*icicles, make a fire, melt, pick apples, rake the leaves, season, snowflake, throw snowballs*	Focus: Suggestion phrases
TOPIC 3 Food, Wonderful Food!	Unit 5	Listen and visualize	*exotic fruits, garlic, kimchi, kiwi, papaya, red peppers, spices, watermelon*	Give a group presentation
	Unit 6	Listen to classify and categorize	*can of tomatoes, carton of juice, chili peppers, cinnamon, honey, melon, spinach, yogurt*	Focus: Transitions
TOPIC 4 Animal Planet	Unit 7	Listen for opinions	*beak, eagle, escaped, feathers, flamingo, hummingbird, peacock, swans*	Persuade
	Unit 8	Listen for attitudes	*endangered, gorillas, in the wild, pandas, paws, penguin, rhinoceros, wings*	Focus: Persuasive phrases
TOPIC 5 Our World	Unit 9	Listen for problems	*diverse, immigrants, Kenya, Nepal, New Zealand, Peru, Russia, the UK*	Talk about problems
	Unit 10	Listen for solutions	*castle, citizen, Italy, Japan, palaces, tower, tradition, Turkey*	Focus: Intensifiers
TOPIC 6 Let's Do Better!	Unit 11	Listen for gist	*awful, furry, metal, plastic, rubber, silk, sticky, wood*	Tell a personal story
	Unit 12	Listen for the theme	*cotton, full, glass, playful, polluted, shout, sound, whisper*	Focus: Past continuous